REAL STORIES OF SPIRIT COMMUNICATION:

When Loved Ones Return After Crossing Over

SpiritStories.com

Copyright © 2004 Angela Hoy

ISBN 1-59113-442-0

All rights reserved. No part of this publication may be reproduced, stored in a retrieval system, or transmitted in any form or by any means, electronic, mechanical, recording or otherwise, without the prior written permission of the author.

Printed in the United States of America.

Booklocker.com, Inc.
2004

Some names have been changed to protect individuals' privacy.

REAL STORIES OF SPIRIT COMMUNICATION:

When Loved Ones Return After Crossing Over

Angela Hoy

SpiritStories.com

With Gratitude

This book is dedicated to the loved ones of the contributors, those who have "crossed over" and then returned, giving us a glimpse of the world they now live in, and the world we will all live in, with them, someday. You will not only be inspired by the stories herein, but will also be enlightened about common occurrences that most people are afraid to talk about.

The photographs featured on the cover of this book are the actual pictures of loved ones appearing in our stories. See the following four pages for their names and corresponding chapter numbers.

I also dedicate this book to the contributors themselves, many of whom said that writing their stories helped them with their grief. They know they have helped other searching souls by doing so!

To my dad, David Jerome Phillips (see #5 on the following page), who died when I was five years old. He doesn't come around like he used to, but I think of him often and look forward to being in my daddy's arms again someday.

To our friend, Bob Freiday, who died while this book was being written. We'll miss the belly laughs, Bob, but we'll see you soon!

And to my aunt, Barbara Greathouse, who also died while this book was being written. Diabetes and strokes took many things from you, but nothing could ever diminish your sense of humor. Your courage is an inspiration to all who knew you.

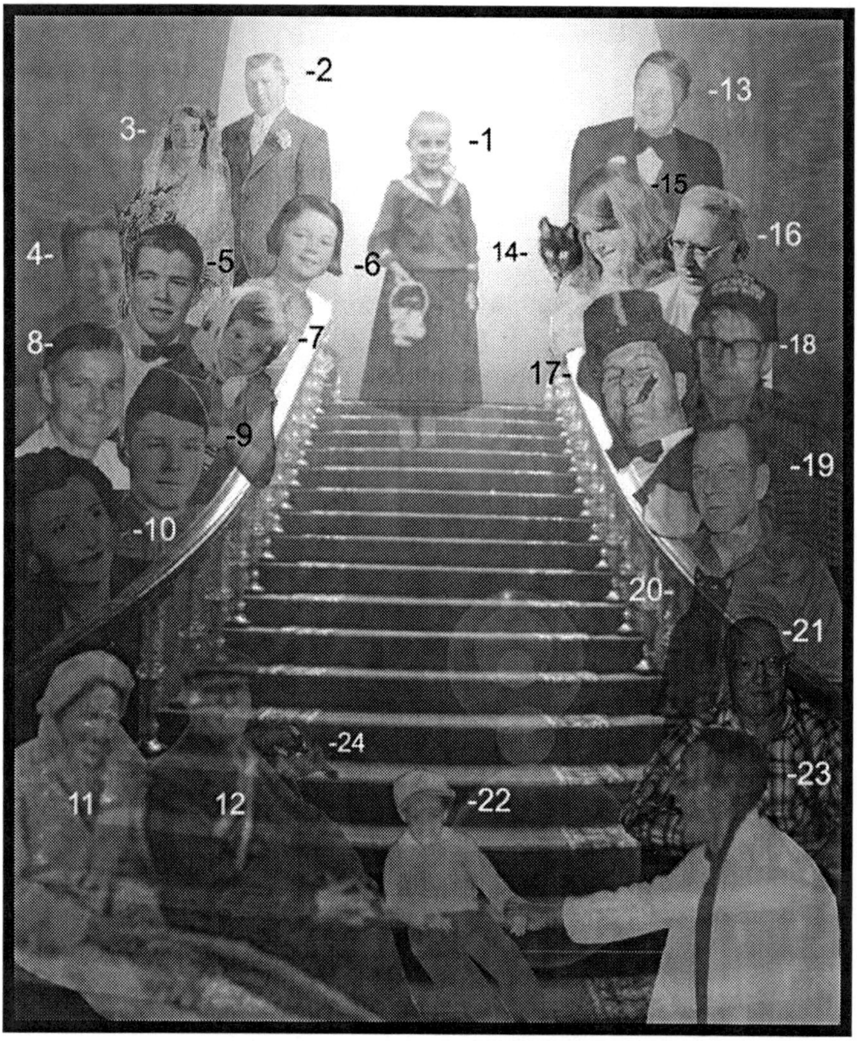
-2
3-
-1
-13
-15
4-
-5
-6
14-
-16
8-
-7
17-
-18
-9
-19
-10
20-
-21
-24
-23
11
12
-22

FRONT COVER PHOTOS

1. Irenke Szilak Balazs - Chapter 12
2. Herbert Daige - Chapter 20
3. Helen Jane Daige - Chapter 20
4. Henny Madsen - Chapter 27
5. David Jerome Phillips - Introduction
6. Charlotte Grisdale - Chapter 35
7. Heide AW Kaminski - Chapter 17
8. Dalton Williams, photo 1 - Chapter 1
9. Dalton Williams, photo 2 - Chapter 1
10. Bubbie - Chapter 15
11. Henny Madsen - Chapter 27
12. Erik Madsen (Henny's husband) - Chapter 27
13. Louis Braunstein - Chapter 19
14. Felix - Chapter 8
15. Diana Thistle Tremblay's sister - Chapter 37
16. Diana Thistle Tremblay's father - Chapter 37
17. Uncle Charlie - Chapter 33
18. Dalton Williams, photo 3 - Chapter 1
19. Robert Arthur Kampa - Chapter 24
20. Yappy - Chapter 18
21. Borden Clark - Chapter 6
22. Sabrina Zackery - Chapter 34
23. Sabrina Zackery's father - Chapter 34
24. Midnight - Chapter 25

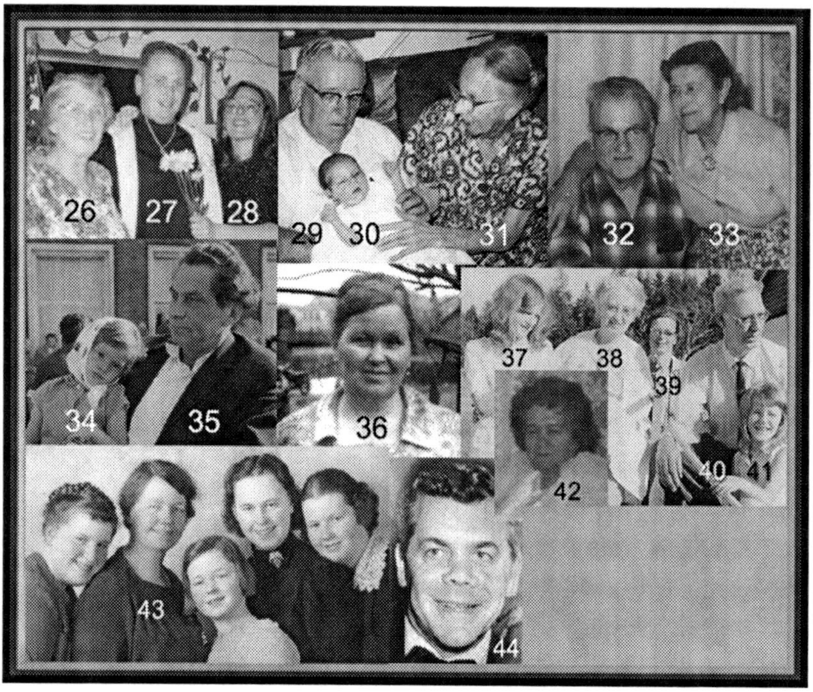
26
27
28
29
30
31
32
33
34
35
36
37
38
39
40
41
42
43
44

BACK COVER PHOTOS

26. Henny Madsen - Chapter 27
27. Michelle Porter's brother - Chapter 27
28. Michelle Porter - Chapter 27
29. Ray Stone - Chapter 3
30. Mark Perrin - Chapters 3 and 4
31. Lynn Stone - Chapter 3
32. Dandad - Chapter 35
33. Nang - Chapter 35
34. Heide AW Kaminski - Chapter 17
35. Reinhold Wegner - Chapter 17
36. Praskovya (Panya) Ivanova - Chapter 22
37. Diana Thistle Tremblay's sister - Chapter 37
38. Diana Thistle Tremblay's grandmother - Chapter 37
39. Diana Thistle Tremblay's aunt - Chapter 37
40. Diana Thistle Tremblay's father - Chapter 37
41. Diana Thistle Tremblay - Chapter 37
42. Doris Buckingham Menzies - Chapter 7
43. Mama Nana and daughters - Chapter 36
44. Jack Lionel Cole – Chapter 31

Contents

Introduction xiii
My Story xx
Medium or Charlatan? xxxiv
Our Stories 1
1. Daddy's Favorite Song 3
2. Unspoken Last Words ARE Heard! 6
3. Grandparents Care For Grandchildren in Heaven 11
4. "Imaginary" Friends 16
5. Jonathan and The Gray Kitty 19
6. A Message No One Else Could Decipher 21
7. My Guardian Angel 23
8. Felix the Cat 27
9. Leaving Baysha 30
10. Returning to Say Goodbye 33
11. Amy's Last Words 39
12. Mother's Message 43
13. Culinary Cravings and A Broken Bucket 49
14. I Love You — I Always Will 54
15. We Are All Eternal Beings 66
16. I'm Okay! 74
17. A Father's Love 78
18. Yappy 81
19. Dad's Protection 89
20. When Spirits Use Signs 91
21. They Come to Take Us Home 96
22. Prayers Are Heard 99
23. "I Saw Daddy!" 102
24. Dad Returns With Advice 109
25. Midnight's Last Visit 116
26. Heeding Dad's Warning 118

27. Moster Henny's Ring 120
28. It's Not What You've Been Taught to Believe 123
29. Nona's Promise 126
30. She Implored Me Not to Be Sad 132
31. "Mommy, I See Jack!" 136
32. We're Just on Different Sides of The Door 140
33. Bye, Bye, Charlie 146
34. The Reason I Came to This Earth 155
35. You Must Go Visit Your Grandmother 159
36. This Is As Far As I Can Go With You 162
37. I Told You So 164
38. Always There When I Need Him 168
39. The Toy in The Boot 173
About Angela Hoy 183
Do You Have a Story to Share? 185

Introduction
Angela Hoy

"*Mom, Mom, I saw him! I saw Daddy, Mom!*" (Chapter 23)

"*You must get in touch with your father.*" (Chapter 12)

"*There stood Bruce, in the corner of the shower, staring at me.*" (Chapter 16)

"*There, blocking the front door, stood Dad, dressed in his gray slacks, cream-colored, button down, short-sleeved shirt looking like he did in the pictures from the 1950s, not the 90s, when he died.*" (Chapter 26)

"*Mommy, I see Jack!*" (Chapter 31)

"*I listened to him say how he never left my side for all these years, how every time I wondered if I were making the right decision, he would show me a sign. I listened to him say how peaceful it was on the other side...*" (Chapter 34)

"*(Heaven is) nothing like you may begin to imagine, nor is it anything like you have been taught to believe it is.*" (Chapter 28)

~~~~~

I was raised knowing there is life after death, but believing that most people end up in hell. So, from an early age, I feared God (which no child should have to do!). At the age of five, my father, David Jerome Phillips (see photo 5 on page vi), died. Shortly thereafter, he started coming to me in dreams. I, of course, thought these were just dreams. Nobody ever taught me that spirits may come back to help us, so it never occurred to me to take the dreams seriously or to even mention them to anybody, not even to my mother.

I'd been taught in church that communicating with spirits was "evil" and only "demons" would be encountered if you actively participated in that kind of nonsense. (And God have mercy on your soul if you ever touched a Ouija® Board!)

I bet many of you were raised the same way. Until recently, I was terrified of death and what might or might not be beyond. I mean, what if the Muslims were right? What if I was the wrong religion? What about the people in African tribes who live their entire lives without bibles or "proper" religious training? Did they all go to hell just because they were born far away from all the preachers in the world? What if the Jews were right and we Christians were all going to burn in hell? And who was this Buddha guy?

How could we possibly know if we're the one "right" religion, and why does every religion dictate that members of every other religion are going to hell? The older I got, the more I thought about this and realized, if God loves us more than we even love our own children (a love so strong I can't even fathom its intensity), he would never banish us, no matter what we did wrong, even if our parents or our society raised us under the "wrong" religion.

So, I created this book for people like me, people who are afraid of death or who fear, for whatever reason, they will never see their loved ones again after leaving this world. And, hopefully, by reading these words, you will learn more about how to either communicate with your loved ones who have already crossed over or to simply recognize when your loved ones are trying to communicate with you.

Subtle Signs
Our loved ones often use subtle signs when trying to tell us they're visiting. Sometimes, these signs are so subtle that others think we're imagining them or putting too much emphasis on natural occurrences. For example, someone may

see a blue butterfly in winter and believe it's a sign from their aunt, who loved blue butterflies. Another person may hear their recently departed spouse's favorite song on the radio played several times in one day. There are many people who receive subtle signs from loved ones, and some of these signs are valid forms of communication. However, because these signs can be interpreted differently, this book focuses on more direct forms of spirit communication, such as voices and visions.

> *Perhaps Heaven is the way we want it to be; whatever our heart desires.*

Ha Ha's in Heaven

In some of the stories featured here, you'll notice that a loved one's sense of humor survives with vigor! Not only do quick-witted loved ones enjoy making us smile once again when they come to visit in spirit, but we even find that some people who were quite serious and stoic when here with us are much more laid back and happy there. Humor in Heaven is quite cunning, as many of you may already know.

Contact Can Be Frustrating

While you're reading this, please know that different forms of spirit communication work for some people, but not for others. For example, I failed miserably at Automatic Writing (until I stopped trying so hard). I can easily see spirits in my mind's eye when meditating (more about that later), but I assumed for a long period of time that those spirits existed only in my imagination. So, I ignored my visions and tried methods that others used successfully—not realizing I had already discovered my "gift." There are a variety of ways to contact your loved ones who have died. If something doesn't work for you, try something else. We all have different strengths and gifts. Repeatedly attempting something that is just not working

> The thought that all communication from Heaven just stopped one day just doesn't make any sense, does it?

for you, or something that you think should work because it's working for someone else, will only lead to frustration.

Why Is It So Hard to Believe?

I often hear negative words about my research and personal spiritual experiences from skeptics, strangers, friends, and even family. I find it disconcerting that the majority of people in the world believe in a supreme being and the afterlife, and they believe in the angelic and spiritual visits detailed in the Bible, the Koran, the Tanakh, and other historic texts, yet they scoff at the possibility of spiritual visits happening today.

All religions tell stories of spiritual visits from angels, departed loved ones, and even God himself. Yet, people who have not experienced their own visitation think it's impossible to receive communication from the other side in today's modern world. Why? Why would God turn his back on us and remain silent today when life experiences, exposure to other faiths, and even technology make it so hard to believe in Him sometimes? The thought that all communication from Heaven just *stopped* one day just doesn't make any sense, does it?

When I was a little girl and attending Confirmation classes at the United Church of Christ, I asked my minister, point blank, about those poor people in African tribes. How would they get to Heaven when nobody had ever taught them about Jesus? He answered, "Well, God expects everyone to understand that there is something greater than themselves and to believe in that Being."

But, I thought, he'd been preaching to us every single week for as long as I could remember that you have to believe that Jesus was the Son of God in order to get to Heaven! Now he was telling me that those African people just had to believe in "something." Huh? What was going on here?

Even at such a young age, I understood that this minister, this messenger of God who I had been taught to respect and believe, had just contradicted the main message he'd been preaching to me and to other parishioners for years.

Why do some people who have returned in spirit describe valleys and meadows while others describe buildings and roads? Why do some people report being met by loved ones who passed before them, while others state they were met by Jesus, or another prominent soul from their own religious beliefs? Perhaps God wants to comfort us when our souls are abruptly sucked out of our bodies and brought back home. Perhaps Heaven is the way we want it to be; whatever our heart desires. This theory, which I believe to be true after my research and experiences, has answered a lot of questions I had about the variety of experiences people report from the afterlife. If Heaven **is** how you want it to be, it would be a glorious place for **all of** us. Imagine what you want Heaven to be like for you. I **believe** that what you just thought about is exactly what you **will have** when you die.

If you still doubt **the existe**nce of spiritual contact in the modern world, let me **ask you** this. Why, after thousands of years of direct contact with **people** on Earth, would God just abandon us? Why would **God talk** to shepherds, but not to me? Why would angels visit **people** 2,000 years ago, but not visit people now? What has **changed**? Nothing at all. Heaven hasn't changed. We have.

If you believe in angels, why is it so hard to believe that angels still bring messages and protection to people today? If you believe that some biblical figures returned with messages for their families and others after their deaths, why is it so hard to believe that our loved ones who have crossed over don't occasionally stop by for a visit as well?

REAL STORIES OF SPIRIT COMMUNICATION

> Heaven hasn't changed. We have.

As you'll read in the stories here, spiritual visits have not stopped. Visits from Heaven are as prevalent today as they've been throughout history. The only difference is that nobody talks about them anymore and, when someone does experience something they can't explain, they doubt themselves. Why? Because that's what society has taught us to do. Even people who don't doubt themselves, who know that what happened to them was special and spiritual and real, keep their mouths shut. Everyone's too afraid to be labeled a freak.

I'm one of those people. When I read about the hate mail some people receive after writing books that contradict organized religion, I almost wrote this book under a pen name. But what kind of message would that send to others like me, people who want to come forward with stories of love and healing from grief, but who are afraid of society's judgment?

If we keep discouraging those who have been blessed with visits from sharing their experiences, our doubts and judgments hurt everyone. Each telling of an angelic or spiritual visit brings hope to those who have not yet learned how to recognize visits from their own loved ones, and the lessons taught by our loved ones who have crossed over should be shared with as many people as possible. Spirits who come back with lessons to teach have so much wisdom to share! For our own comfort and happiness, we need to learn how to listen to them, and we need to learn how to share our stories without worrying about the opinions and judgments of others.

One night, shortly after my minister confirmed my suspicions that the church teaches you what they want you to hear, not necessarily what is right, I was on my knees in my bedroom, praying. I asked God, "Why don't you come down and see people anymore?"

When Loved Ones Return After Crossing Over

I immediately felt a presence so powerful in my bedroom that I started crying. I knew it was God, and I was terrified! My heart started beating so hard I could hear it in my chest. His presence faded as quickly as it had come, leaving me stunned and humbled. I was so terrified that I didn't immediately understand that he hadn't just stopped by for a visit, but he had also answered my question.

Years later, this memory is as fresh in my mind as if it had happened yesterday and, when I was older, I finally understood the true meaning of his message. When that small, insignificant 12-year-old little girl in Texas got down on her knees to ask God why he didn't come to visit people anymore, his answer was, quite clear.

"I do."

My Story
Angela Hoy

When I was five years old, my father died of cancer. Shortly thereafter, I started dreaming about him. The dreams lasted well into my teenage years, when they, eventually, stopped. In the dreams, my father would always give me advice. While growing up and experiencing these dreams, I thought they were just dreams. Nobody had told me that spirits come to visit in dreams, so I never suspected they were anything more than my imagination.

Years later, I realized that the advice he gave me in my dreams was far more mature and contained more detailed information than my imagination was capable of producing at that age. Sadly, it was only after the dreams had stopped that I understood my father had come to tell me things he wasn't able to tell me in his lifetime, things I wasn't old enough to understand when I was only five. Now, however, rather than regret the misunderstanding, I cherish the fact that my father never left me.

I do still dream about my father on occasion, but now he doesn't speak. He just nods his head and smiles at me. I'd like to think that's his way of telling me he's proud of the woman I have become.

When my daughter started talking at the age of two, she occasionally mentioned odd things, such as the woman with the long blonde hair who liked to sit in her bedroom. Ali saw people we couldn't see, but nobody seemed to appear with any regularity. I believed her, but didn't know if the sightings were her imagination or not. I certainly didn't mention the occurrences to family members or friends, fearing they would treat her differently or even make her feel like they didn't believe her. I didn't spend a great deal of time pondering the occurrences and just accepted them as part of Ali's world. After

When Loved Ones Return After Crossing Over

all, many children have imaginary friends, right? But, Ali didn't play with hers or even talk to them. They just appeared to come and go, and they became a normal part of Ali's life; no different than one of us walking through her room.

When we moved to Maine four years ago, we purchased a home that was built in 1896. Strange things happened on occasion, and then Ali and, eventually, Frank (her younger brother) saw "ghosts." When I experienced my first spirit (I don't think they're "ghosts"); well, the only way to describe my reaction was utter shock, followed by panic. I was sitting in our office (most occurrences in our home seem to occur in Frank's room, the office, and the mudroom), talking on the phone with my mother. Richard was out running errands and the children were in school, so I was alone. Richard's office chair was turned away from me. I noticed, out of the corner of my eye, the chair moving back and forth, back and forth. The movements weren't small at all. The chair was turning left to right, in wide movements, but not all the way around. I thought Ali's cat, Blotch, was in the office with me. So, after hanging up the phone, and seeing the chair still moving, I leaned over and swung it around to pet the cat...and the chair was, you guessed it, empty. I started shaking and my eyes filled with tears and I said, out loud, "I can't see you, but I know you're there!" Then, I ran out of the room! I told Richard about it when he got home. He, of course, thought it was the wind (the windows were closed), but I knew I'd had a visitor. There was no wind, no earth movements, and no cat. There was just no other explanation for what I saw.

Prior to last month, Zach, our oldest son, had never seen anything he couldn't explain and was a firm skeptic. He plans to be major in engineering and his beliefs are grounded in math and science, Zach is very logical in his thinking and not religious or spiritual at all. In the past, if I talked about our visitors in front of Zach's teenage friends, he'd roll his eyes and turns red with shame. Well, he's a believer now! After years of disbelief, Zach saw Jonathan standing by the door in the mudroom, but that wasn't all. He also felt a cat rubbing against his leg one day and, when he reached down to pet it, discovered there wasn't anything there. That's a sensation Ali and I experience frequently.

Max's room is situated between the upstairs hallway, the master bedroom, Frank's room, and Zach's room, so it has four doors. Recently, Frank (age 11) walked from our room into Max's room and saw Richard leaving the room from the door on the opposite side. Frank then turned left, toward the hallway, and jumped when he saw Richard walking down the front stairs. Frank yelled, "Mom! I just saw Daddy going through Max's room, but then he was on the stairs!" Frank was shocked and excited, but not frightened at all.

Richard, my husband, is also a skeptic, but an open-minded one. He does believe there are things we don't understand and can't see in this world, but he requires concrete proof before he will accept anything as fact. It's actually comforting to have a skeptic in the family to keep us grounded when things get just a bit too weird. Richard has never seen anything, but has "felt" odd at times. He's asked me repeatedly if I was turning off his computer late at night and if I was leaving the closet door open. It wasn't me, nor was it the children because they were in bed. And, while each incident can easily be blamed on electricity and drafts, the occurrences are random and unexplainable. So, Richard is open to the possibility that somebody he can't see might be playing games with him. (In Chapter 5, Ali writes about how she has seen Jonathan sitting at Richard's computer.)

We were eating dinner recently with friends when they confided that their daughter had seen the spirit of a woman in our house when she had slept over with Ali one night. She said she was lying in bed in Ali's room when, through the bedroom door, she saw an elderly woman walking down the front stairs.

When Loved Ones Return After Crossing Over

Several years ago, when we lived in Texas, a young girl was kidnapped within a few miles of our home. It was the lead story on every news station and in every newspaper for several days. It was heartbreaking, and I couldn't get her out of my mind. I had three young children at that time, and I was just sick about the situation.

On my lunch hour one day, I was sitting in my car at a stoplight and, in my mind, but with my eyes still open, I saw the little girl's body lying at the base of a large drainage pipe. The vision was very disturbing. I was also disturbed by the fact that my imagination could conjure up something that gruesome when I was simply listening to the radio and thinking about which fast-food restaurant to stop at for lunch.

The next day, they found the little girl's body lying in the opening of a drainage pipe. They suspected she had been murdered and put in a drain and that her body had traveled through the pipe to where it was discovered. The news showed footage of the drainage pipe. It was the pipe I'd seen in my mind. When I saw the pipe on TV, I got very upset and called my mother, frantically telling her what I'd experienced.

She asked, "Did you tell anybody at all about this?"

"No way! People would think I'm either sick or crazy," I replied.

She said that was good because she didn't want the police to think I had anything to do with the child's disappearance. I hadn't even thought about that possibility. I, of course, didn't tell anyone else about that until 2003, when something else strange and disturbing happened.

On February 1, 2003, Richard and I woke up and turned on the TV to watch cable news, as we always do on weekend mornings while reading the paper and drinking coffee. On Fox News, they were covering the space shuttle landing. I used to work in the aerospace industry and shuttle landings just aren't as exciting for me as they used to be. Just as I was about to change the channel on the remote, a voice in my left ear quite clearly and calmly said, "It's going to crash."

I felt completely foolish and wondered why my morbid mind was thinking such a terrible thing. I even said to myself, "Where did that come from?" I changed the channel. A few minutes later, Richard said, "I'm hungry. Let's go eat breakfast."

We went downstairs and, while I was cooking eggs, Richard was in the dining room watching television. I then heard him yell to me, "The space shuttle blew up!"

I ran to the dining room and was completely shocked and deeply upset. I started shaking and told Richard about the voice I heard in the bedroom. I then woke up the children to tell them what had happened (not about the voice in my ear, but about the shuttle exploding), went to the bedroom, started crying, and called my mother.

Mom suspected that I heard something on television in the background about it exploding and that my subconscious was playing tricks on me. I tried to explain to her that the shuttle wasn't yet missing when we were watching the coverage on Fox News while lying in bed. She didn't believe me. Our daughter, Ali, came into the bedroom and heard me telling my mother what happened. When I hung up, Ali hugged me and said, "There's nothing you could have done to stop it, Mom."

Ali, who was 12 years old at the time, and who had been seeing, hearing, and feeling things the rest of us could not understand for her entire life, knew instinctively that my reaction was due to guilt, and she knew exactly what to say to make me feel better.

I could no longer ignore the fact that something exists that is not part of our visible world. Did everybody have experiences like this, but just not talk about them? Did other people ignore these startling coincidences, visions, dreams, feelings, and voices and assume they were fiction, as I'd always done? One way or the other, I wanted to know the truth. So, I started the research that led to this book, but with an openly skeptic mind.

When Loved Ones Return After Crossing Over

I read numerous articles and bought dozens of books on psychic phenomena and spirit communication, written by a wide range of people, from scientists to self-proclaimed psychics and mediums to professional skeptics. During my research, some people (including my own family members!) accused me of dabbling in the occult. I ignored them and continued my studies. I researched everything from spirits to ghosts, mediums to psychics, Wicca to Islam, Judaism to Christianity, near death experiences, astral travel (which I was never successful with), meditation, chakras, and more. I learned about things I'd never even known existed and met people I thought were enlightened and others whom I thought were downright crazy. And, finally, in an attempt to establish communication with these spirits instead of just occasionally hearing and seeing them, Ali and I attended mediumship classes. Now, that was truly enlightening and a lot of fun!

The views I express here are the opinions I have formed after completing my research. Yes, my research is finished. I have collected enough proof, from my own research and experiences, to confirm that; yes, we do go on. There is a Heaven and it's only a breath away. And our loved ones do communicate with us. We just need to learn how to listen!

Everyone is Intuitive
Most people with psychic gifts claim that everyone has psychic abilities. For example, you've probably heard of women's intuition. Well, everyone is intuitive, not just women. Have you ever felt that your child or other loved one had been injured and learned later that they *were* really injured at the exact moment you became concerned a problem might have occurred? Have you ever been humming a tune, turned on the radio, and found it playing? Have you ever known who was on the phone when it started ringing or been thinking about someone only to have them call you, drop by, or run into you at the store a short time later? Have you ever known, in your mind, that a relative died

before you actually learned they had died? How many times in your life have you experienced something that can't be explained and thought, *that was really odd*? Just like some people must take piano lessons for years while others can play instantly by ear, psychic or intuitive abilities vary by person. Some people may experience simple déjà vu throughout their lives while others may have the ability to predict the future from the day they learn how to talk. Some people may be able to subtly pick up on the feelings of other people while others may experience the actual physical pains of those around them. And some children have imaginary friends who may, as you will read in this book, simply be deceased loved ones coming by for cherished visits.

~ ~ ~

On the very first night that my daughter, Ali, and I started mediumship classes, after a relaxation meditation, I saw people (spirits) standing behind the real people in the room with us. I, of course, thought these people were figments of my imagination. And, boy oh boy, was my imagination going nuts! One spirit fellow, in particular, was really funny. He was standing behind a woman named Suzie and waving an American Flag, a big one. I kept trying to ignore him. I mean, he wasn't really there, was he? He was just in my mind, right? He kept waving that darned flag and was looking me right in the eye and trying to get my attention. I didn't say a word. I knew nobody else could see him. It was kind of like when you have a song stuck in your head. You keep trying to forget about it, but it keeps playing through your mind, over and over again. Well, the flagman was just not going to go away, no matter how many times I told myself he wasn't real. He stood there behind Suzie, waving that flag, over and over again. He was pretty hard to ignore, but I kept pretending he wasn't there, because I truly believed he was not there.

I, of course, kept my mouth shut and didn't tell anyone in the room about the flagman that night.

The next week, the group leader called on me specifically and asked if I felt, saw, or heard anything. I had recovered from my feelings of stupidity and shame and, knowing these people didn't really know me or any of my friends or family, or even my last name (thank goodness!), said, "Okay, this is gonna sound really stupid, but here goes."

I told them what I'd seen the week before, about the man standing behind Suzie, very insistently looking me in the eye and waving a large American flag. My face was burning in shame by the time I finished, and I hoped they'd all be very kind and not make me feel like more of a fool. Suzie, not at all fazed by my story, said it sounded like I was seeing her father. She said if he knew about the (Iraq) war going on, he'd be glued to his television (hence the flag). I was shocked and pleasantly surprised (though I still thought it had probably been my imagination). Then she said, "But he's still living."

Um, huh?! She then said he was very ill and, from what I understand of the conversation, I don't believe he was conscious at that time. I was too embarrassed to ask any questions.

Many people who have experienced this type of phenomena believe that a person's soul can leave their body if it's ready, despite how long doctors and science are able keep that body alive. Now I, personally, don't think God makes people in comatose states wait for years to be happy and free while their families and doctors force food and oxygen into their broken bodies. While their bodies may continue to show life on those monitors, in reality, nobody's home.

While I was quite pleased that I'd seen something that could be verified, despite the affirmation, I was still skeptical. I believed that, in all likelihood, the flagman had only existed in my imagination and that the similarities were simply a coincidence.

I had one burning question when I started studying mediumship that no book answered. Do mediums really see a flesh and blood person or is a transparent soul standing there? Or are they just seeing something in their mind? If the people I saw were real souls, then the latter is a better description. I could see the flagman standing there, making gestures, but I didn't have to look directly at him to see him. I knew, in my mind, what he looked like and what he was doing because I could see him with my eyes closed, too. I could also see directly through him because he didn't appear to be a concrete person. But, of course, I wasn't trying to see through him and I knew, instinctively, that if I stood up and waved my hands where he was standing, I'd not feel anything. But, again, I was too stunned and embarrassed at that moment to start formulating scientific theories about the matter this vision was created from.

What does it mean when a medium says 'I can see it in my mind's eye?' I've come up with what I hope will give you an idea of the meaning of "in my mind's eye." Seeing something in your mind's eye is like dreaming, but with your eyes open. You can see something or someone there and your eyes are open, but at the same time, you know they're not really appearing in any concrete form. It's like seeing something with your eyes closed, but opening your eyes and still seeing it.

For example, picture a school bell in your mind. Your eyes are still open as you're reading this, but you can still see that school bell in your mind. If you close your eyes, you can still see that school bell. Yes, it's as simple as that! That's how it is when you see spirits, and why it's so hard for beginners to determine if the visions are their imagination or not.

If you see a spirit, and if you're a skeptic like me, you then wonder if what you saw was real or not. In fact, all mediums occasionally question the validity of what they see, even veterans. Since the imagination can create something as detailed as, say, a man waving a flag, mediums seek confirmation of the people and things they see in order to separate their imagination from real visions. Confirmation from those around you is the only way to know if your visions are, indeed, real spirits or people.

Later in that same meeting, another person popped into my mind's eye. I saw a short, very thin, young woman standing behind Jacques. She was in a nurse's uniform and had dark hair. The primary things I noticed about her were the nurse's uniform, her brown hair, and the fact that she was so petite. Since my imagination had so quickly conjured up another very detailed vision, I started to consider the possibility that perhaps it wasn't my imagination after all. That thought excited me.
    I decided to assume the young woman was real. "What now?" I thought. Then I wondered if seeing a nurse meant that Jacques was going to get sick. So, I didn't say anything.
    After the meeting, I asked the group leader, "What do you do when you think a message is negative?" She said that our interpretation might be wrong. While there are certain specific things a person may see, feel, or hear that should not be shared, if a vision is not understood, it should be shared.
    During the next meeting, while still not certain if the young woman I'd seen had been real or not, I told the group about the nurse behind Jacques. Jacques smiled and said the woman I saw was his daughter. The description was perfect, right down to the brown hair, petite size, and profession. Yes, she's a nurse!
    Okay, I was on a roll! I thought, "I can really see dead people!" But, my excitement was instantly extinguished when Jacques said, "But, she's alive."
    What? Again?!
    The leader explained that, sometimes, intuitive people may feel and see the energies of loved ones who may be close to or even thinking about the people we're with.
    Arrgh! I wanted to see spirits, not living people! I see people all the time! I wanted to see "beyond the veil!" (What I really wanted was proof that there really was life after death, and

seeing absent but living people was *not* what I anticipated when I signed up for that mediumship class.)
    Unfortunately, when receiving contact from the other side, you don't get to pick and choose what you see, hear, and feel. It just happens. But after several classes and a lot of meditation, I now know that's the way it's supposed to be.

Over the next few weeks, I kept seeing spirits, different ones during each class. Ali was having success, too, but much more than I was! She had numerous visions of places and occurrences that were confirmed by the other class members as being accurate. She could feel the emotions of those around her, describe someone's childhood home, know things about their past by touching something they owned (psychometry) and, yes, see spirits and even give brief messages to the people they came to visit. And, while Ali and I were stunned by the things we were seeing and learning, the veterans in the class didn't seem at all surprised by anything that happened.

After watching my fellow class members experience a variety of gifts like Ali's, I started trying to see, feel, taste, hear, and, in any way, sense emotions, words, feelings and actions—anything other than seeing spirits; spirits who wouldn't talk to me, even in my mind, no matter how many questions I asked them. I was frustrated that none of them interacted with me whatsoever, but just stood there, looking quite content. I grew so frustrated that I stopped looking for (and started ignoring) the spirits I was seeing. And that was easy since I only saw them after meditating anyway (except for one incident in a grocery store, but that one didn't talk to me either). I figured since that mediumship stuff wasn't working (because the spirits didn't do what I wanted them to do), I'd explore other forms of psychic ability, such as automatic writing and psychometry.
    The problem was, no matter how hard I tried to turn off the mediumship part of my experiences (the spirits) and turn on some psychic abilities (being able to read the people around

me), nothing worked. I still saw spirits, but they were always silent. I wasn't feeling, seeing, or hearing anything else when I tried to will myself to do so. Oh sure, I'd see images flashing in my mind, but almost none that I was capable of interpreting. I certainly couldn't tune into anybody and see anything about their future, nor could I tell them anything about their past.

One odd thing that did happen that I hadn't read about was the increase in occurrences of unexplainable things after you start meditating on a regular basis (I only did it weekly). I started to see flashes of floating lights at all hours of the day, whether meditating or not. A friend thought I was having small strokes and my mother told me to go to the doctor. My ophthalmologist gave me an odd look and said she'd never heard of the lights I described seeing, but didn't order any further tests. Class members said the lights were a classic description of orbs.

I started to see auras around people when I wasn't trying to see anything, and I even started to hear voices in quiet rooms when I was involved in everyday activities, such as cleaning house. (Richard, my dear, skeptically open-minded husband, said with a smile, "None of them tell you to kill me, do they?") I even wrote down what the voices were saying for a while, and they appeared to be bits and pieces of conversations, never complete sentences. I thought perhaps my mind was echoing what I'd heard from other people, television, and even the radio. After writing down their words for several days, I can tell you with certainty that they do not come from my daily experiences. Some words and terms were definitely not from anything I'd watched, heard, or experienced. One very specific medical term, which I'd never heard before, was so clear in my ear that I wrote it down and looked it up on the Internet. And it was a real medical term, but something I'd never heard or read about before.

After weeks of attending classes and trying to do what I'd seen other people do (without success), while trying to ignore those visions of spirits who wouldn't talk to me anyway, I decided to, once again, study those people who I saw but who didn't respond to me. Maybe I had done it all wrong. Maybe a person or a book could help me communicate with these spirits. Maybe I'd been trying way too hard to force something to happen when I was just supposed to relax and watch it unfold? So, I decided to, once again, pay attention to the spirits in the room and to just let them be there. If they didn't want to talk to me, that was fine. Maybe no words or thoughts were needed.

In our next meeting, I saw a very rotund woman standing behind Jacques' wife, Linda. She was, again, quite large and wearing a long, white dress. She had gray hair, and the style led me to assume it was in a bun, but I couldn't see the back of her head. I remembered to ask her, in my mind, if she had a message or needed anything. She just smiled and nodded her head. She seemed quite friendly and tranquil. Even though I didn't know if she was real or not, for some reason, her presence made me feel warm and happy inside.

Then I saw a dog standing by Belinda, another group member. He was really fluffy, black and white, and a fairly medium-sized dog. He looked very soft.

After about 20 minutes, I finally got up the nerve to say something. After describing the woman in white, Linda said I was seeing her aunt, who had worn all white when she was helping people—all white because she was a nun. Her aunt had also come by for a visit when Linda had a reading by a medium the previous week. Linda keeps a picture of her aunt in her living room and they were very close when her aunt was still alive, and obviously still are.

The dog was Belinda's daughter's dog that had died the previous fall. After seeing two spirits in one night and receiving confirmation from my classmates, I was beyond excited! Seeing visions is one thing, but getting confirmation that you're not hallucinating is incredibly fulfilling. During our many meetings, I only saw one spirit that nobody could identify, that of a young boy. All the other spirits I saw were recognized by the class members they were standing behind.

Medium or Charlatan?
Angela Hoy

Finding a medium is a tempting and comforting idea for those experiencing grief after the death of a loved one. While you may learn to meditate (some people don't need to meditate to see spirits) and experience things that may or may not be your imagination, it may still be tempting to try to find someone who can confirm or deny your experiences, or even open a clear channel of communication between you and your loved one.

You have no doubt read about the frauds in this line of business. How do you know if a medium's message is real or not? If you listen to a medium and approximately 85% of what they say can be applied to most people, chances are they are grasping at generalities. If most of what they say is very specific, and can't be applied to most people, then they may actually be getting real messages…but not always. Be wary of mediums who may have "plants" in their audience. (A plant is a friend or associate of the medium that sits in the audience and pretends to affirm everything the medium says.) Be wary of mediums who ask questions and get to know people in the audience before or even during readings. They are probably fishing for information. Also, be very wary of mediums who are extremely dramatic and theatrical and/or use elaborate props. This type of behavior and atmosphere is not necessary.

The only true way to know if a medium is giving a real message is if that message is for you or someone you know (not a stranger), and if that message is very specific and wouldn't be understood or recognized by the vast majority of people.

If a medium states they have your mother there (if you're of a certain age, it's easy to guess if your mother or a "Mother Figure" has passed over already), and that she had pains in her chest (lots of people die of heart problems!), or lists two or three different general ailments, or seems to make repeated and vague guesses as to the "messages" they're receiving...well, that person is either a new medium, a poor medium, a good medium who's having a bad day (it happens), or a fraud. If the medium can't provide you with very specific information (without asking you any questions), they should be avoided. While it may be tempting to try to "help" the medium by providing information, don't. You should never give a medium any assistance and only answer their questions with a yes or a no (when asked if you understand a message they have given you). Good mediums don't ask for information; they provide it. And, good mediums don't try to interpret the messages they receive; they simply give the information as it comes. If they truly are receiving messages from your loved one, they shouldn't have to ask you any questions.

If you don't understand a message that is given, it's okay to say so. Sometimes, the spirit who is communicating with the medium can provide more detail, or can convey the message in a different way. Believe me, your loved one doesn't want to bless you with a visit, only to leave you confused. So, it's okay to say, "No, I don't understand. Please provide more information."

Should you ask the medium questions to relay to your loved one? Sure, but wait until it looks like the reading is coming to an end. And, don't provide so much detail that the medium, should they be a fraud, can use to fool you into believing something that they're creating. Instead of asking detailed questions that would only require general yes or no answers, ask general questions that require detailed answers. For example, instead of saying, "Dad, the police said you ran that stop sign and that's why you were killed. Is that true?" Say, "Dad, tell me more about your death. I need to know what happened." Again, if the medium can provide detailed information that can't be recognized or understood by the vast majority of the population, your loved one may really be coming through for a loving chat.

REAL STORIES OF SPIRIT COMMUNICATION

I once saw a medium give messages to a woman and her daughter from the woman's late husband and his mother. The medium not only knew the exact occupations of the father and his mother, and exactly what the family did as a memorial to the husband, but she also knew their names. Some people claim that the spirits themselves must be good communicators to get messages across clearly to mediums. Perhaps, but a medium should not pretend to know the message or interpret it in any way. The message should come straight from the departed loved one.

One night, Richard and I attended a service where a medium was speaking. She was communicating with the family of an elderly gentleman who used to wear his false teeth upside down as a joke. I considered that message very specific and certainly not something that would apply to 85% of the population. I was impressed, until Richard leaned over and whispered, "Could be a plant."

The medium approached me later and asked, "Have you recently given someone a haircut?" Richard and I looked at each other. His eyes were wide open and my jaw dropped. A comment like that also would not apply to most of the population, and it blew me away. You see, our baby, Max, had needed a haircut for quite sometime, but I just couldn't bring myself to cut his baby locks off. Finally, the week before we were sitting there, listening to that medium, I gave Max his first haircut. It was a very bittersweet moment for me because Max was transformed from a baby with wavy locks to a little boy with a bowl haircut. I didn't say anything to the medium, of course. I just shook my head yes to affirm that I did understand the message.

The medium continued and said my three grandmothers thought the haircut was "very sweet." Now, how many haircuts would be considered very sweet? That definitely would not apply to the majority of the population! She gave me, personally, more very specific messages, some that I could never confirm, along with some general things that I dismissed because they could be applied to just about anyone. But, the haircut message really shocked us both!

Mediums, even good ones, have their bad days. Some days they get every message right, and sometimes either the spirits aren't conveying their messages in a way the medium can understand, or the medium just isn't hearing or seeing them clearly.

Several months after our first professional medium experience, I took Ali to that church, and the same medium was there. I was very excited because she had delivered so many very specific messages to people the previous time. However, I was gravely disappointed when she repeatedly "missed" throughout the evening. In fact, if I hadn't seen her at work before, I'd have thought she was a fraud. That's how bad it was. She read Ali and me and the only thing that she may have come close on was talking about the spirit that Ali frequently sees in our house, Jonathan. But, it may or may not have been him. She batted zero with me. I didn't recognize and could not confirm anything that she said to me that evening.

Of all the psychic phenomena I've studied, contact with departed loved ones holds the most sincere interest for me. My experiences and research has led me to seek out other people who have been spontaneously contacted by their loved ones in spirit. The people whose stories appear here are not practicing psychics or mediums. They are ordinary people like you and me who were not actively seeking contact with the spirit world, but who were pleasantly surprised (and, of course, occasionally frightened) when the contact occurred. Here are their stories.

Our Stories

1. Daddy's Favorite Song
Sandy Williams Driver

My daddy loved country music. He used to tell me stories about his family gathering around their old Zenith® radio back in the early 1930s and listening to the latest bluegrass tunes each Saturday night on the live Grand Ole Opry® radio broadcast.

The late 1940s brought the haunting voice over the airways of the man my daddy always proclaimed to be the *best country music singer of all times*, Hank Williams. The legendary performer was no relation to my father, Dalton Williams (see photos 8, 9 and 18 on page vi), even though both men were tall and thin.

As a child, I often sat beside Daddy as he listened with a hint of a smile to one of the many Hank Williams records he owned. I remember watching the small black circle spin on the turntable and listening respectfully to the enduring voice tinged with a slow, southern drawl and a touch of static.

Over the years, Daddy replaced his LPs with 8 track tapes and then, a little later, with small cassette tapes. He always bought every Hank Williams selection he could find. In the mid-1990s, my sister bought a CD player for Dad. He liked it immensely and, of course, the first CD he bought was *Hank Williams Greatest Hits*.

He thought it was grand that he could push a button and immediately hear a specific song anywhere on the disk. Daddy loved all the songs recorded by Hank Williams, including *Your Cheatin' Heart* and *Kaw-Liga*, but his favorite tune was *Hey Good Lookin'*, which was number 13 on the CD. He would sit and listen to it over and over again.

A few weeks after my daddy died on May 28, 1999 from cancer, my mother brought a trunk full of boxes over to my house. She had kept a few of Dad's personal belongings, but had decided to give me some of my father's memorabilia.

> At exactly midnight, my husband and I were abruptly awakened by the blaring sound of our stereo in the living room.

We sat down on the floor of my den and began sifting through the memories of Daddy's life. In the bottom of a large box, underneath a stack of neatly pressed handkerchiefs, I found an old, faded, and yellowed newspaper article dated 1953. It was clipped from a tabloid in Montgomery, Alabama and told the distressing news of the death of the beloved country music singer, Hank Williams, at the young age of 29.

Mother had no idea where Daddy had gotten the newspaper. Because he thought it was important enough to keep, I folded it carefully and placed it in my scrapbook for future generations to read.

In another box, I found the *Hank Williams Greatest Hits* CD my dad had listened to so many times. I smiled and asked Mom why she didn't want to keep it for herself.

"That CD player stopped working months before your daddy died and I haven't gotten around to buying another one," she told me. I had no idea their CD player was broken and thought it was sad that Daddy didn't get to listen to his favorite CD during the weeks before his death.

After Mom left, I put everything back in the boxes and left them in the den. It was getting late and my breaking heart just couldn't hold up to opening another container of reminders of Daddy that day.

I went to bed around 10:00 p.m. and fell into a deep sleep. At exactly midnight, my husband and I were abruptly awakened by the blaring sound of our stereo in the living room. We jumped out of bed and raced down the hall expecting to see one of our young sons up on a stool messing with the knobs on our sound system, which was on the top shelf of our entertainment center.

When Loved Ones Return After Crossing Over

The darkness of the living room greeted us and sent us racing to find the light switch. The bright glow revealed no playful children, just an empty room. My husband rushed over to the stereo and reached up to turn the power off, when I stopped him.

A chill ran down my spine as I pointed to the open CD case lying on a middle shelf of the entertainment center. I picked it up and gasped aloud when I closed it to reveal the title *Hank Williams Greatest Hits*. I stared, open-mouthed at my husband as number 13, *Hey Good Lookin'*, started to play over again.

The children had been awakened by the loud music also, and stumbled into the living room with sleep filled eyes. "What's going on?" they asked.

I really had no idea how to answer their question. I knew, as the last person to go to bed that night, that Daddy's CD had been left packed inside a box, downstairs in the den. Two hours later, it was in the living room, in the CD player, and set to play a specific song repeatedly.

My husband gave me a warm smile before kneeling in front of the children. "It's just your Paw Paw listening to his favorite song."

Today, three years later, I still have the Hank Williams CD sitting beside my stereo. I carefully take it out of the case and play it in its entirety at least once or twice a month. I always stop on number 13 and play it a couple of extra times just for Daddy.

Sandy Williams Driver lives in Albertville, Alabama with her husband, Tim, and their three children, Josh (16), Jake (14), and Katie (12). She writes a parenting column, Tots and Teens, for The Sand Mountain Reporter, *in Albertville, Alabama, and her short stories have been included in numerous publications including* Mothering, Parenting with Spirit, Home Cooking, Your Family, ByronChild, *and* Australian Family *magazine.*

2. Unspoken Last Words ARE Heard!
Suzanne T. Jackson

When Hurricane Hugo reared its windy head in our inland community, that event seemed minor compared to the emotional blow our high school had been hit with. It was 1989, and I was a blooming 15-year-old girl. My friends and I were so excited about going to a bigger school with bigger people and bigger prospects. Out with the old and in with the new became our new motto. But as children can continue their unrelenting ways, even in their teens, most of the old that would be forgotten would include most of the kids we had been friends with since kindergarten.

Too young to have a driver's license, most of us continued to endure the yellow-diesel guzzler. No one wanted to ride the bus in high school, so having your own car, or at least knowing someone who had his or her own wheels, was the only way to be seen in the school parking lot without embarrassment. The first week of school was the time when we were all getting situated in our routines of who was going to remain our friends throughout the next three years. I made the conscience decision to exclude any and all of my past friends that lived on the "other side of the tracks." It was popularity and name brand all the way for me. One guy in particular, Cliff, who I had known since the second grade, and probably someone I had been a girlfriend to at one time or another, made an attempt to pass over to the cool side with me.

During an afternoon bus ride home, Cliff tried talking to me. That didn't seem strange to him. After all, he had known me since I had pigtails and crooked teeth. In an out of character response, I completely ignored any conversation with Cliff. He was, in my head, from the "other side of the tracks."

I could tell that my icy reaction to Cliff was hurtful. My rejection showed on his face with embarrassment and confusion, I wanted to tell him how sorry I was and be pals with him again, but I couldn't. I was too afraid that I wouldn't be accepted if I interacted with one of "those" kids.

Another bus-riding sufferer was Stephanie. She was tall and thin with baby soft blonde hair and a personality that could light up a room. Stephanie was a girl from the right side of the tracks, so everybody wanted to be friends with her. To my advantage, Stephanie and I had been friends as long as Cliff and I had known each other.

Going into the second week of our high school saga, one afternoon, all the kids noticed that Stephanie and Cliff weren't on the bus. Some kids started saying that Cliff had gotten his license late last week and he was driving home today. Instantly, that allotted Cliff with cool points. He would be one that we could potentially catch a ride with. But that didn't explain where Stephanie was. She hadn't missed the bus in years, if ever.

Suddenly, some kids started yelling and carrying on saying they saw Stephanie in Cliff's car, and that they were just ahead of us. What!? How could that be? A cool kid riding in a car with a not-so-cool kid? Without any explanation, we knew that Stephanie was just using Cliff so she could look even cooler by avoiding a tortuous bus ride home.

For the next five minutes, most all of bus number 361's occupants continued to discuss the freshest gossip. Suddenly, Cliff's car hurled by us with a loud roar. Clearly his "new" wheels had no muffler. Loss of cool points—yet Stephanie's reputation remained unaffected. Some kids hung out the bus windows, cheering Cliff. Up ahead, you could see Stephanie standing up through the sunroof, waving her hands.

We envied Stephanie's advantage of getting home faster than us. Where she would be home in only 10 minutes, we still had 30 minutes to go.

I was going home with a friend of mine that day. Her bus stop was located by her father's convenient store. In my selfish ways, all I could think about was getting free gum, drinks, or chips. As we stepped off the bus, two ambulances went roaring by us. My stomach began to cramp; something it always did whenever an ambulance went by. In my typical consoling way, I thought, I hope it's just for a pregnant woman who can't get to the hospital.

My friend and I proceeded with our afternoon, talking about who was cool, cute, and in style, and predicting who would end up being whose girlfriend this year. Her mother came home within the hour. Maybe, at this point, we were trying to ignore the anxiety she was obviously displaying, as if wanting to tell us something. When my friend's older brother came home a few minutes later, it happened. They sat us down, side by side on the couch, and told us there had been an accident. Being young and naïve, we'd never really experienced any "accidents" before. So, being prepared was not something we would be able to pretend.

Who? Where? When? How? We both thought it, but couldn't ask. Then there it was; Stephanie and Cliff had been in a car accident and neither one of them survived the crash. My friend didn't take the news well and began to weep loudly. I just sat there in silence. I've always been the type of person to not get all worked up about something I hadn't actually seen.

The week finished with sadness and silence throughout the halls of our school. This time was supposed to be fresh and new, vibrant and memorable, but not memorable in this way. My parents allowed me to attend the viewing of Stephanie and Cliff; both in separate parts of town, but they didn't allow me to attend either funeral. My parents knew that this emotional blow was an overload to my mind.

Two days after both teens were buried, news of Hurricane Hugo's approach began to prepare our town for something that had never happened in its history. Some people left their homes, others boarded up windows. Most all of us collected tubs and milk jugs of water. Pantries were stocked with extra food and batteries, candles, and matches. Not knowing what to expect, we toughed it though. I slept through most of the ordeal, only to wake up long enough to move downstairs.

When Loved Ones Return After Crossing Over

As the days passed, the mourning numbness I'd experienced for Stephanie and Cliff began to fade. Overwhelming guilt began to sit on my shoulders like a metaphysical monkey. How

> *"I just wanted to tell you goodbye one last time and tell you that I forgive you."*

could I have been so mean to Cliff? Why did I have to be so hurtful to him when I had no idea how long he was going to be here? I became depressed, saddened by my shallow ways. Nothing seemed to help shake my feeling of just wanting to tell Cliff goodbye one more time. I should have said it to him that last day he rode the bus. I missed him.

After three days of no power, our water supply went dry and we packed up and went to my grandparents' house down the road. That night, as I was trying to go to sleep, I still felt guilt that was untouchable. But, when I finally went to sleep, something occurred that I had never experienced before. When I awoke, I was crying hysterically. My mother was at my side, comforting me. She knew I had been upset over my young friends' short lives, but she didn't realize that my tears weren't of heartbreak, but of relief.

During my slumber, I began an incredible dream. I was suddenly walking down a hallway at my school. Crowds and crowds of people were all over the place. Walking through the sea of students seemed almost impossible, but through the crowd emerged a face I recognized. A friend of mine came up to me with a look of sheer excitement. She seemed almost too happy to speak.

"Cliff is here! Cliff is here! He wants to talk to you!"

For reasons only dreams can explain, I was escorted deeper within the crowd of people. Conscientiously, I knew Cliff was dead, but it seemed odd to question my friend's persistence. And there he was. Cliff was standing in the middle of a crowd that seemed to avoid a one-foot radius around him. He was wearing a tie-dyed t-shirt; they had become the staple part of his outfits. He looked melancholy, but a little bit anxious. And then he spoke.

"I just wanted to tell you goodbye one last time and tell you that I forgive you."

In the dream, I didn't talk back, but I do remember being overjoyed by being able to have that one last time to tell my friend goodbye. And then, just as I had been escorted into the crowd, I was being escorted out of the crowd. Someone was comforting me as I continued down a hall that became less populated. That was when I woke up with tears of relief and content.

Fourteen years later, I still recall that event, dream, visit as if I had it just last night.

Suzanne T. Jackson is a mother of two boys and a wife to "the perfect man." A college graduate from Lenoir-Rhyne College in North Carolina, Suzanne has been writing since she was 14 years old. Although she has had other experiences with friends passing away and visitors in her dreams, the visit from Cliff has always affected her more deeply than the others. For more information about Suzanne and her writing services, please visit her website at http://www.geocities.com/lrcbsn_01/usingtherightwords.html.

3. Grandparents Care For Grandchildren in Heaven
Lynn R. Hartz, Ph.D.

Grandma was a very special person in my life. Her name was Lynn (see photo 31 on page viii) and I was named after her. We were always close and, as a child, I would spend days and hours with her. She taught me to sew and let me play the pump organ and piano. When I had a problem, she was there.

Grandma had been a schoolteacher and was delighted when I went to college. However, she was even more delighted when I married and started my own family.

My first baby, Nell, was born on my grandparent's fiftieth wedding anniversary. That, needless to say, made her a very special little baby. Nell was born in August in Arizona and I brought her to West Virginia at Christmastime. Grandma couldn't wait to put Nell in her lap so she could "nurse her baby."

My husband, Bill, died a year and a half later. He was a very special person to Grandma, not only because he had married me, but also because he was a staunch Republican (like she was) from West Virginia, which was something of an oddity.

My second child, Hope, was born six weeks after my husband's death. Of course, I moved back to West Virginia. I felt a need to be near my family. Shortly afterward, I married again and had another child, Mark (see photo 30 on page viii).

By then, I had three children under the age of three. My new husband had opened a business and I was working as a full-time counselor. Family life was sometimes difficult to manage.

"Grandma, could I bring the babies down for a little while? I need to pick up some groceries and I can't take all three of them with me."

REAL STORIES OF SPIRIT COMMUNICATION

I knew the answer would be "of course." Though my shopping trips never took more than an hour, it took two trips from the car just to get all three children into their house. That was the beginning of several Saturdays that the children spent a small amount of time with their great-grandparents.

"Now, Grandma, don't pick up the babies. Let Granddaddy hand them to you. They're too heavy for you to lift," I'd say. I'd always make her promise not to pick them up. Granddaddy (see photo 29 on page viii) would always agree to make sure she didn't lift them. I would come back and, of course, Grandma would have one of the children on her lap. Granddaddy would sit one of them on her lap for her to cuddle and love. I always felt warm and happy when I came to their house to pick up the children.

Mark was learning to eat with a spoon. My husband would hand him the spoon and put it in his right hand. Mark would transfer it to his left hand. My husband would say, "You can't play basketball and golf if you're left-handed, Mark." He was serious when he would say this.

But I was delighted. Mark was a "lefty!" I was a lefty, Grandma was a lefty, and my brother was a lefty, too! We were all excited. "Lefties are smarter than righties," we'd tease. Mark was definitely a "lefty" and definitely smart. He was so smart that he sucked his right thumb so that he could use his left hand to do other things. Grandma was delighted!

The three little children were looking forward to Halloween. Nell remembered a little about Halloween because she had been in nursery school the two previous years. Hope and Mark did not understand Halloween and really didn't care.

Each child had a costume. Nell was going to be Cinderella, Hope was going to be Raggedy Ann, and Mark was going to be Raggedy Andy.

On Halloween night, I took the children down to "Trick or Treat" my grandparents. They always enjoyed the children and had such great fun when they would come for a visit.

My grandmother was beginning to be very frail. The children did not understand that she was not as strong as other grownups that they knew.

The children rang the doorbell. "Trick or treat!" Nell said. Hope didn't say anything. Mark held out his pumpkin, pulled open the door, and said, "Candy," as he went into the house. Nell had on her mask, but Hope and Mark had long since done away with that foolishness.

Grandma was delighted. She said that the best part of Halloween was seeing "her babies." Mark saw Granddaddy and almost knocked Grandma down as he ran in to see him.

"Grandma," I said. "You sit down and let me hand Mark to you."

"Okay, Granddaughter," she said. "You know I'm not as strong as I used to be."

So, I sat Mark on her lap. He put his thumb in his mouth and cuddled up to her for a little while, but only a little while. Granddaddy brought him some candy, so he wriggled off Grandma's lap so he could peel the paper off the candy and eat it.

Nell promptly went over to sit on Grandma's lap for a few minutes. Although Nell had been born on my grandparents' fiftieth wedding anniversary, Mark had missed their anniversary by only one day. Mark was going to do his own thing!

When Nell, Hope, and I returned to West Virginia from Arizona after my husband's death, Nell had been confused about the grandmothers. I had told her that this was Great-Grandma. She had, from then on, called her *Great*-Grandma, with a strong emphasis on the Great. Grandma loved it. The other great-grandchildren soon picked up calling her *Great*-Grandma, but it was always special when Nell said it.

Mark was not talking a lot, but as we were leaving that night, I asked the children to say goodnight to Great-Grandma and Granddaddy. That was the night that Mark first said "Great-Ganma." Happiness lit up my Grandma's face, and she seemed almost like a little child, she was so pleased.

> *I'm not as strong as I used to be, and I'll be going soon."*

Two weeks later, Mark was dead. He had found matches and the house had burned to the ground. My aunt and uncle went to tell my grandparents about Mark's death. Grandma was visibly shaken.

Grandma came to the funeral home. Mark's body was in a closed white casket.

"Grandma," I said. "You have no business being out in this weather! It's rainy out!"

"But Granddaughter, you knew I'd be here. He was mine, too, you know," she replied with tears in her eyes. And I knew she was right. We put our arms around each other and cried.

After Mark died, I'd go visit my grandparents often. I always felt comfortable talking with them. One day, Grandma put her arms around me and said, "I'll be going soon myself, you know. I know that your other grandmother is there with Mark, but I'll be there to take care of him, too."

I cried. "Grandma, I don't want you to talk like that. You'll be here for a long time yet!"

"No, Granddaughter. I'm not as strong as I used to be, and I'll be going soon."

I left with tears in my eyes and a lump in my throat. I knew what she said was true.

Six months later, Grandma was gone. I felt as though a part of me had died with her. My whole insides ached with longing for her, my baby, and my husband. "How unfair death is!" I thought. "Why do all the people I am closest to die?" Of course, I knew that everyone died, but I was weary.

A few months later, I awakened from a dream in the middle of the night. I had a vision of Grandma and Mark. I saw Grandma holding Mark. I talked to her. I told her not to pick up Mark because he was too heavy for her. I offered to put him in her lap just as I always did, but this time she wouldn't allow it.

"No, Granddaughter. You don't need to do that. You see, he's not too heavy anymore."

Lynn R. Hartz, Ph.D. lives in Charleston, West Virginia and is a retired psychotherapist. She is the author of And Time Stood Still, *a novel about the midwife who delivered the Christ Child, and* Club Fed, *the story of her personal experience with the legal system and imprisonment, (both available at http://www.amazon.com), Lynn is also co-chairperson of the West Virginia Poetry Society annual contest. Licensed also as a minister, she has worked with spiritual development, intuition, and religious understanding. She is a member of Unity of Kanawha Valley and the Aquarian Universal Spiritualist Church.*

4. "Imaginary" Friends
Lynn R. Hartz, Ph.D.

When my daughter, Grace, was three years old, it was time for her to begin preschool. She really liked going to school. Every morning when she got up, I helped her dress, and then we would have to help her invisible friend get dressed as well. We helped him put his pants on and zip them up and even helped him tie his shoes. We had to buckle his seat belt in the car and take his blanket to school with us. And we held his hand going up and down the steps to the school.

"Grace," I began one day. "Do the other children know about your friend that we take to school?"

Looking at me as though I were some kind of stupid person, she said, "Of course they do, Mommy. They like to play with him, too."

Well, of course they like to play with Mark, I thought. Mark was the name of Grace's invisible friend.

Several weeks after we had been taking Mark to school with us every day, I sat down on the floor in front of my desk and looked through some old pictures that I had put away.

"Gracie, come here. I want you to see a picture," I said to her. She came close and sat down on the floor next to me. "Look at this picture."

She didn't just look; she took the picture out of my hand. "That's him! That's Mark!" she told me excitedly.

"I know," I replied. "That is Mark. Mark was your brother who died before you were born." She was young, so I'd not yet told her about her brother who died before she was born. But I had often wondered if her friend, Mark, was her brother (see photo 30 on page viii).

"I used to play with him before I came to live with you and be your little girl," she said, matter-of-factly.

I then told her about Mark and that he had died before she was born, and that I missed him very much. He was only 2½ years old when he died, and he was never old enough to attend preschool, but he always wanted to go with his older sisters. I wondered if he was just a little envious of Grace having the opportunity to attend preschool, and he just decided that he would go with her, since he didn't get to go by himself.

> *"I used to play with him before I came to live with you and be your little girl,"* she said, matter-of-factly.

Mark continued to go to school with Grace until the Christmas holidays. When she returned to preschool after the Christmas holidays, Mark was no longer with us. Perhaps he didn't need to go with her anymore, or perhaps she didn't need for him to go with her after that; it really doesn't matter. What is important is that Grace's relationship with Mark served a very important purpose at that time in her life, and he was as real to her as any person who has a body that is visible.

As children grow and their minds become more cognitive, as they develop their intellect, they frequently stop communicating with spirits. Grace, however, is an exception to the rule.

We had a wonderful dog that died, and she has seen and felt his presence in our house. One night, in the very coldest of the winter, Grace was sleeping with me in my bed.

"Mom. I think Noodles is here," she said. Noodles was the name of our long-legged, beige-eared poodle.

"Grace, I think you're right. I just felt something on my feet," I said. I had experienced Noodles at various times, and he still liked to sleep on my feet at the foot of my bed just as he had when he was living.

"Isn't it nice that we can still be friends with Noodles, even though he isn't always here?" Grace said. I answered her affirmatively, again marveling at the ability this child had to perceive things beyond the physical realm.

We have had experiences with other spirit animals in our house. For a while, I thought I was "seeing things," not just

> As children grow and their minds become more cognitive, as they develop their intellect, they frequently stop communicating with spirits.

seeing spiritual things, but becoming somewhat disoriented and delusional. I kept seeing a black cat in the house and we had never owned a black cat. We had other cats, but never a black cat. Not only could I see it at times, I could also hear it because it sometimes would make audible "meows" and other cat sounds. Frequently, I would look around because I would see a black streak and then it would be gone, or I would hear a sound and look, and there would be nothing there.

As Grace and I were sitting watching television one day, she looked at me and said, "Mom, I keep seeing this black cat in the house. Have you seen it?"

I sighed and said, "Yes. Thank goodness I'm not going nuts. I was beginning to worry about myself! I didn't know anyone else had seen it." Grace's ability to see the cat was validation enough for me.

Lynn Hartz's bio appears in the preceding chapter.

5. Jonathan and The Gray Kitty
Ali Hoy (age 13)

I will remember, for the rest of my life, something that happened not very long ago. It was early evening and my mother had just taken my baby brother, Max, to give him a bath. As she put him into his rocking seat, it broke suddenly, and he went crashing to the floor. After we picked him up and hugged him, my mother said, "Ali, go ask Daddy if he can fix this." I climbed the stairs and asked my father. He said no, it was beyond fixing, and told me to put it in the mudroom, which is right under the office in our house, and which has its own stairway.

So, I went into the mudroom, and there he was. Jonathan. He ran up three steps and turned to look at me in the eye, and then ran up the rest of the steps. This was not my first encounter with Jonathan, but it was the most vivid! I wasn't really sure about what I'd just seen and thought maybe it was my little brother, Frank, playing with me. I called up the stairs, but there was no reply. It turns out my brother and mom were both in the living room. I asked my dad if he saw anyone come up the stairs and into the office. He said nobody had walked through there. That's when I knew for sure that it had been Jonathan.

Other times, I would just get a glimpse of him out of the corner of my eye, sitting at my father's computer or sitting on the couch. Later, I learned that Jonathan was not the only spirit in our house. A little dark, grayish cat was also here with us. I would see him sitting on a windowsill and pass him, thinking it was one of our cats. When I'd reach out to pet him, he would be gone. Sometimes I would see him on the front hallway stairs. My mom and I kept feeling a cat rubbing against our legs. But, when we reach down to pet it, the cat is always gone.

The first night I saw Jonathan was when I was reading in my parents' room. Out of the corner of my eye, where one of the

> Maybe they do go back and forth to the light and we just don't understand how that works

chairs sat, was a young boy with dark hair. Other times, I would see him in the bathroom while I was taking a shower. Jonathan and the cat are not the only spirits in our house. I have also seen our old dog, Baysha. Seeing Jonathan and the animals startles me sometimes, and sometimes I still get afraid even though I know they won't hurt me. Some people ask me how I know his name is Jonathan. One day, I asked him his name, and that's the name that popped into my head.

I have told Jonathan and the cat to go to "the light" several times, but they always seem stay here. Maybe they have a job to finish, or maybe they do go back and forth to the light and we just don't understand how that works.

Ali Hoy, age 13, is the daughter Richard and Angela Hoy. She has been describing things others can't explain since she started talking at the age of two. She previously attended a private Catholic school in Bangor, Maine, and often questioned why her personal experiences with spirits do not conform to the beliefs of the Catholic Church. Ali enjoys reading, painting, and writing and feels that seeing spirits is just a normal part of life.

6. A Message No One Else Could Decipher
June Gallant

My father (see photo 21 on page vi) passed away on February 29, 1988 after a long illness. Five days later, on the 5th of March, I received a phone call from my cousin asking me to come over. She said something had happened that she didn't understand and hoped I could help her. Mary Anne told me that the previous evening, she dreamed that she had a visit from my father. In her dream, Daddy had come into her kitchen and stood by the table. She could feel that he was very happy and was laughing as he did something very strange. She said he looked directly at her and, with his right hand, touched his throat, his heart, and his ankles. He was wearing the brown suit that he had been laid to rest in. Could I, she wanted to know, help shed any light as to what this all meant?

As I sat there slack-jawed, it didn't take an expert to know that she had hit a nerve. He was passing on a message that not one other living soul could decipher other than my mother and myself. We lived in a rural area, a good half-hour's drive into the nearest town. On the morning of Daddy's passing, Mom had asked me to go upstairs with her to help choose the appropriate wear for his final rest. The funeral director would be arriving shortly to pick them up.

As we put his things together, Mom, in her distressed state, couldn't locate Daddy's new tie; we had to substitute his second best. Being a laborer all his life, he didn't own a new hanky for his lapel or a new pair of white socks. I lived next door and my husband happened to have both of these items in his drawer, so I borrowed them to complete Daddy's attire. Naturally, this is not a subject that needed to be discussed with anyone, including other family members. No one, other than Mom and myself, knew about any of this. I have absolutely no doubt that Daddy appeared to Mary Anne to tell her that he was happy and, since she and I were close, he knew exactly who

> *He was passing on a message that not one other living soul could decipher other than my mother and myself.*

she would call. He touched his throat (tie), his heart (hanky), and his ankles (socks), knowing full well that this would be indisputable proof of his visit from the other side.

June Gallant is a freelance writer and has published short stories and articles in a number of newspapers and magazines. Her work has appeared in print both nationally and internationally. Although she has been recognized for her children's stories, poetry, and nonfiction, June is happiest turning out a good horror story that sends a chill down your spine. She lives with her husband, Rick, in Atlantic Canada where she is currently working on her first horror novel. You can contact June by email at ricardo@nb.sympatico.ca.

7. My Guardian Angel
Carol Roach

I was raised by my grandmother, Doris Buckingham Menzies (see photo 42 on page viii). Neither my mom nor dad had wanted me when I was born. My mom was single and said that she would put me up for adoption rather than keep me. In those days, being a young unwed mother was a disgrace. Strangely, it was my dad who brought me home to his mother and I was immediately accepted and raised by her. I was so loved and protected by her that her own children often felt that she loved me more than them. But I know that it was not true. I just needed more love than them, since I was ignored by my parents.

As I grew up, I knew who my parents were, but I did not see much of either of them. My father stopped seeing me when I was five since he married another woman who didn't like our family. My mom was around sporadically to take me out somewhere, but I never felt comfortable with her. My grandmother was my "Ma," (short for Grandma).

Ma protected me all through my life and she loved me like no one else ever could. My grandmother never left the house in the years that I was growing up. Being alone herself and having lived a life of severe hardship, she was severely depressed. Her link to the outside world was the telephone and the television.

One of my fondest memories of the times we had spent together was sitting down and watching Billy Graham's crusades. I always prayed that Ma would admit that she loved the Lord. She neither encouraged me nor discouraged me from going to church. However, I had met a group of friends that were churchgoers and, at the age of nine, I started faithfully attending Sunday school at a mission. Six years later, I don't really know what happened, but I seemed to have drifted away from church life.

I married and had a son. Both my husband and I started to go to church every Sunday. But then somehow we drifted away as well. In 1980, I was alone with my son. I had just divorced and my grandmother had passed away during that same time. I felt totally alone and isolated.

After the funeral, I wanted to know more than anything else that my beloved Ma was okay. I wanted to know that she was in Heaven and that I would not have to worry. I was hoping that all the years we spent watching Billy Graham together had meaning, and that she was now with her Maker. I needed to know so badly that she was happy! It was almost an obsession with me, and I prayed for a sign, any sign, to know that she was okay.

I had a recurring dream at night where she would come back to me to tell me something, but I could not hear the words and I could not reach out and touch her. The barrier between life and the afterworld was still apparent, even in my dream state. The dream would only serve to torment me further.

So strong was this need to know about her happiness, that I decided to go to church with my young son and pray to God for a sign that she was okay. I went to church for the first time in years and just sat quietly in the pew, listening to the sermon. I had no clue what that sermon was going to be and I don't even remember today what it was all about except for one statement that the minister made. He said, "And all of you out there who are worried about your loved ones who have passed on, do not worry for they are happy." I couldn't believe it; I got my sign!

After that time in church, I felt better. First of all, I had my sign and, secondly, the dreams of my Ma's failed attempt at communication had ceased, for she had found her first means of getting across to me.

I began to talk to her in prayer, and each time that I spoke to her, I would touch the emerald ring that she had left for me. It comforted me. I always wore it and still do, for it is a constant reminder that she is with me now and forever, that she is looking out for my best interests, and that she is keeping me safe from harm's way.

Not long after her passing, we had a transit strike here in our city. Montreal is a city that enjoys four seasons, but having a public transit strike in the dead of winter is not a pleasant experience. Since I was now divorced, I could not enjoy the luxury of staying home to wait it out, so I found myself freezing on the corner of a busy intersection, waiting for a car to offer me a ride.

Even while I was freezing and knew that others had to do the same thing, I was afraid of getting into a car with a stranger. Ma had often told me about the dangers, but I was desperate. My options were limited; it was either go home and lose the day's pay, which I could not afford, attempt to walk to work and risk frostbite, or accept a ride and pray to God that I would be safe. I chose the latter. However, the cars were not stopping for me and I was getting colder and colder.

I decided to touch the ring and asked my Ma to help me. Within 30 seconds of touching the emerald ring, a car stopped for me and drove me to work. It was then that I realized that my Ma was my guardian angel. She protected me in life and she was protecting me in death as well.

There have been numerous other times I asked for my Ma's help when I was stuck or in a jam, and each and every time, all I had to do was touch that ring and lo and behold, I got either what I wanted or a compromise that I could live with. When I think about the outcome of each problem, heavenly wisdom always offered the best solution.

Is my grandmother my only guardian angel? I'm not sure. But as I think now, she is the most prominent guardian angel by far. She guided me through this life and now guides me from the realm beyond this world as well. I believe that I may have a cluster of angels and loved ones that protect me, but I feel my Ma, my guardian angel, will always be the most prominent angel in my life and that of my son.

REAL STORIES OF SPIRIT COMMUNICATION

Carol Roach is a native of Montreal, Canada and has a master's degree in counseling psychology. All aspects of psychology and the paranormal are of interest to her. She loves people and writing and is currently working on her first book.

8. Felix the Cat
Jean C. Fisher

Felix (see photo 14 on page vi) was my long-haired, black Angora cat. I adopted him when I was still in college (he was about a year old at the time) from a young woman who was moving out of the country and couldn't keep him. Felix was one of those animals that many people were drawn to because of his quirky and almost-human personality. He also had a "Peter Sellers-like" gift for physical comedy.

While others of his species could demonstrate their catlike grace by being able to jump up on narrow knick-knack shelves and carefully pick their way around delicate breakables without moving them so much as a hair's breadth, poor "Mr. Felix," as everyone affectionately called him, had been cruelly denied that particular talent!

His attempts at such a feat of agility would invariably result in disaster, as precious figurines clattered to the floor, followed soon, thereafter, by the thud of his stocky body with its thick, luxurious coat of sable brown fur. Immediately, in true Peter Sellers style, he would leap to his feet and then turn and glare suspiciously back over, first one shoulder and then the other, as if trying to catch the culprit who was obviously responsible for pushing him and causing him to fall!

Felix was still with me when I married, got pregnant, and gave birth to my daughter, Carmen. He seemed to love Carmen from the moment I brought her home from the hospital, and would often sleep curled up beside her in her crib. As she grew older, he spent hour after hour just napping near her in her room as she played, chattering away to him the entire time.

I guess Carmen was about 7 years old when Mr. Felix passed away in his sleep at the age of about 18. We buried him on the hill behind the house and held a small ceremony there. Tears rolling down her cheeks, Carmen gathered flowers and laid them lovingly on his grave.

> After a few seconds of silence, I said to her gently, "You saw Mr. Felix, didn't you?"

For months following "the funeral," it seemed to me as though I would catch a glimpse of Felix, as I had a million times, skittering in front of my car as I came down the driveway. Then I would realize this was simply not possible and dismiss the thought.

About six or seven months after Mr. Felix passed away, I was sitting in our living room one afternoon reading a magazine. Carmen was dashing around the room, skipping and playing and dancing, as only young children with all that energy can do. Out of the corner of my eye, I saw her start to run from one corner of the large room to the other. Suddenly, she stopped in mid-stride, on tiptoe, in the middle of the room, flinging her arms out to counterbalance herself to keep from falling. She froze in this position staring intently at the floor in front of her.

As the rest of her body remained in that awkward position, she slowly turned her head to look at me, and I could see that her mouth and both eyes were opened wide in an expression of pure astonishment.

It seemed to me as though she was trying to speak, but was somehow dumbfounded and couldn't find her voice. But she didn't have to say anything at all because I knew immediately, just from the look on her face, what had happened.

After a few seconds of silence, I said to her gently, "You saw Mr. Felix, didn't you?"

Still staring at me with that bewildered look on her face, eyes as wide as saucers, she could only nod her head a couple of times, very slowly.

I continued, "And you didn't want to kick him accidentally, so you stopped short and then realized he wasn't here anymore, didn't you, honey?"

Again, she nodded, closed her mouth, and slowly began to lower her arms.

"It's okay, sweetie" I reassured her, "I still see him, too, sometimes."

Jean is a native of Northern California where she lives with her husband and, of course, her kitty, Plunkett. Aside from her work as a freelance writer (one credit is included in Haunted Encounters, Atriad Press), *she is currently working on a committee to write the 150-year history of Luther Burbank's Gold Ridge Farm where she volunteers her time. Jean also serves as co-president of the Western Sonoma County Historical Society.*

9. Leaving Baysha
Angela Hoy

After a violent divorce from my first husband, I met and married a wonderful man and we relocated to the northeast. Sadly, we couldn't find any apartment complex or rental home that would allow dogs. Cats were fine, but nobody wanted dogs. So, we had to leave our dog, Baysha, with my mother in Texas. I was quite distraught about leaving her on the day we drove away in the moving truck with everything we owned and loved—except our beloved Baysha, who we had saved from the pound as a puppy eight years earlier. She was like another child to me, and I have still not gotten over the guilt of abandoning her like that.

Sure, she was well taken care of, spoiled, in fact, by my mother and the rest of my family. But I know she missed the children and us with an intensity that I will probably never understand. To this day, I still feel tremendous guilt over leaving her behind, and I'm crying again over my guilt and deep sadness as I write this.

I had a speaking engagement in Texas a few months after our move, so I was able to visit Baysha and my family. Baysha was so happy to see me! She jumped and barked and crawled in my lap and didn't leave my side the entire time I was there. I think she thought I would be taking her home with me, back to the three children she'd loved and protected for almost their entire lives. But I couldn't take her with me, and again, my heart was being ripped out, knowing I had to leave her there, once again. On the last day of my visit, Baysha knew I was leaving alone, that she had to stay behind. She whined and cried all day long. And once again, I did the wrong thing. I left her there, knowing my mother would care for her, but not knowing the extent of Baysha's emotional pain nor the extent of the pain I would experience from my guilt for the next several years.

When Loved Ones Return After Crossing Over

By the time we purchased a home, Baysha was too old and ill to make a trip by plane to our new home. She had lost her sight and developed a horrible skin condition that left her scratching continuously

One morning, our son, Zach, came in our bedroom looking very distraught. He said he'd dreamed that Baysha died. The dream was so realistic to him and he was so upset that we called my mom to check on Baysha. Mom said, "Well, honey, she is dead."

My mother and step-dad had finally decided that Baysha was suffering too much from her skin condition to be forced to endure even one more day of physical torture. So they held her tight while the vet put Baysha to sleep. Mom had been trying to find a way to tell us that our beloved Baysha was dead, but she had not yet been able to do it.

Oh, God, how we cried and grieved. I cried because I missed her and, again, from the guilt of abandoning her. To this day, I know that abandoning a member of our family, someone who was like a child to me, was and will probably always be the biggest mistake I ever make in my life. I should have smuggled her into the new apartment and just risked getting caught. Such a fool I was at that time; so intent on following the rules and doing the "right thing." But sometimes the "right thing" is dead wrong when it involves someone you love.

One day, earlier this year, while attending a dinner party, our youngest son, Max (age 18 months at the time), choked on a tortilla chip. While he was trying to breath and I was trying to clear his airway, he started vomiting blood. Richard and I ran out the door, leaving the other children at the party, and raced to the emergency room, almost having an accident on the way. It was 20 degrees outside and we hadn't even grabbed our jackets. The hospital was only five minutes away, and we knew it would be faster to get him to the hospital ourselves than to wait for an ambulance.

Thankfully, Max was fine. By the time we got to the hospital, he was breathing normally again. His airway was clear and they determined the tortilla chip had cut his tonsil, which is what caused all the blood. We returned to the dinner party, shaken, but relieved.

Later, as we were getting in our van to leave, I looked down and was absolutely stunned speechless when I saw Baysha standing next to me, looking up at the van door, waiting for her turn to hop in, just like she'd always done in Texas. I pointed and moved my mouth open and closed a few times before the words finally came out. I said, "Baysha is here! Baysha! It's Baysha!" By the time I finished, she was no longer visible and I, nor Richard or the children, could see her anymore. But, I knew she was there. I even said, "Come on, Baysha! Up!" when I crawled in the van, so she would know I had seen her.

Nobody questioned me, and the children seemed thrilled that Baysha had dropped by for a visit. I can't adequately describe the comfort her visit brought to me. First, I knew Baysha had shown herself to me to let me know she'd been there with us on a night when I thought my baby was going to choke to death. Second, she's not mad at me for abandoning her for the last year of her life (though I still live with the guilt).

Baysha showed up another time, shortly thereafter, in our upstairs hallway, and confirmed my suspicions that she is, indeed, dropping in for visits, still loving us, and still protecting us.

10. Returning to Say Goodbye
Ed Bonapartian

As far as phone calls go, I'm always leery of the ones that arrive late in the night. In my life, they always seem to be a harbinger of bad news. That night it was Charlotte, my mother-in-law, and that call was no different. When I heard her voice, I knew that bad tidings were arriving once again. She told me that Sandy, her companion and a close family friend, had just died.

There wasn't much else that she could say. The news wasn't unexpected since Sandy had been taken to Hospice just that morning. But I also knew from experience that you can never adequately prepare yourself for the emotions that come during a loved one's passing. As I listened to the grief etched in her voice, I closed my eyes, brought an image of Sandy into my mind, and mentally wished his spirit well, wherever it may have gone on its next journey. He had fought a hard battle against cancer but, in the end, his body had simply given out.

As the family gathered at Charlotte's house the next morning, I sat in the kitchen sipping my coffee while staring at a picture of Sandy perched on a living room shelf. Since he had been a companion to Charlotte for close to 20 years, I had over a decade of memories to look back on. Even though we were not related by blood, Sandy was always considered a member of the family through his love for Charlotte. An Italian immigrant who had come to this country in 1968 with nothing more than the shirt on his back, he had worked hard to live the American dream as he and his brother-in-law started an auto body repair business, which slowly grew over time.

Tall and wiry, Sandy had the large, rough hands of a laborer and the dry wit of a comic tinged with a spirit of mischief. In our family, Sandy had always been known for his love of playing cards. It was his passion in life, next to his prized vegetable garden. Often, I would arrive at Charlotte's house to find him on the front porch or at the kitchen table dealing out the cards for another Poker game, as he and his friends taunted each other about their card skills with an Italian dialect that few could understand.

As I sat there looking at his picture, one memory stood out in my mind. It was the memory of a dream he had shared with Charlotte a few months before his death. The dream came at a time when his body was weak, suffering the effects left by the radiation treatments, which caused him to spend most of his days sleeping.

In his dream, Sandy finds himself healthy and free of the pain that had manifested itself in his waking life as he sits at a table playing cards. He sees that all his close friends and family are there, surrounding him with smiles and laughter, as they celebrate the joy that can only be found in long friendships. In this card game, Sandy is king. Every hand is a winning hand, and no one can come close to beating the cards he holds before him. As the dream ends, Sandy is left with a clear memory of that card game. Now, thinking back on that dream, I knew that his dream had been a healing dream, a message to both Sandy and our family that all would be okay after he passed. However, I also felt that it was a dream that needed to be told again, now, to leave an image of Sandy in our hearts that we could hold on to as we dealt with our grief over his passing.

Later that morning, we made arrangements at a local funeral home for Sandy's burial. Since we would be holding a memorial service for him, I decided to honor his dream of the card game by using it as a sort of eulogy, which I could read out loud during the service. I figured this would give friends and family a fond memory to remember him by.

After we got home, Charlotte asked me to take Sandy's clothes over to the funeral home. As she handed them to me, she looked around the room as if concerned she might have forgotten something. This gave me a sudden insight. I asked her to give me a deck of Sandy's cards, the ones he used during his card games. As she handed them to me, I could see her eyes fill up with tears. In those cards was a lifetime of memories for her. Gently, I told her that we

> *Our dreams cross the bridge between the living and the departed and, in doing so, often leave us with a way of saying goodbye that we never expected.*

were going to send Sandy off right; that we were going to honor his dream of the card game by putting a deck of cards in his shirt pocket, the same way he had always carried them around when he was alive. For me, it was my way of honoring his memory and saying goodbye.

A few days later, the priest of the church where the service was to be held rejected the idea of me giving a eulogy during his memorial service because I was not a member of the church. My initial reaction was one of anger. I'm a real stickler for honoring dreams but, in this case, I realized my frustration with the church was not going to get me anywhere. Instead, on the day of his service, one of my sisters-in law, Shelby, gave a short but very moving eulogy. I realized this was her way of honoring his memory and saying goodbye. Life goes like that sometimes; what you think should happen doesn't, but what *needs* to happen does.

Our dreams also work like that. They cross the bridge between the living and the departed and, in doing so, often leave us with a way of saying goodbye that we never expected. But that bridge works both ways, in that it allows the departed to say their goodbyes to us as well.

In the ensuing months, it was apparent through our dreams that Sandy was not going to leave without saying his goodbyes also. A few weeks after his memorial service, I received another phone call from Charlotte. I had been in a hurry to leave for an appointment; however, as soon as she said I was

> *It is often the feeling in our hearts that tells us much more than our rational minds will ever know.*

the only person she could talk to, I stopped dead in my tracks. Something in her tone of voice told me that I needed to listen very carefully to what she was about to tell me. Originally a bit skeptical about my involvement in dream work, she now felt that no one else would believe her experience from that morning.

She had awoken a bit earlier than her alarm was set for and, as she lay in bed in that twilight zone between sleep and being fully awake, she heard a most beautiful melodic sound, as if someone was playing a musical instrument she had never heard before. Looking over in the direction of the sound, she realized it was a row of metal hangers that were hung on a small rack that Sandy had used for his clothes. They were swaying as if moved by a gentle breeze, and something in the movement and sound immediately brought a strong feeling and image of Sandy to her mind.

Now fully awake, Charlotte spoke out loud, "You old son of a gun. You wanted me to know that you were okay, didn't you?"

Since there had not been an open window in her room or anything else to explain the hangers' movement, a feeling in her heart told her this experience had been his way of letting her know he was doing well. Sandy had never been one to directly talk about his feelings when he was alive. If he wanted you to know how he felt about something, it was often expressed in his actions rather than words. But Charlotte could always feel his love for her behind those actions, and now he played a song for her when her attention would be most receptive, in that place between waking and sleep, before the waking mind could merely dismiss it as coincidence. It is often the feeling in our hearts that tells us much more than our rational minds will ever know.

When Loved Ones Return After Crossing Over

In the spring after Sandy's interment, my wife mentioned that she had a vivid dream where she and Sandy were dancing together alone in the cafeteria of the church school she had attended as a child. Since my wife always enjoyed dancing with Sandy at social occasions, I told her I wondered if her dream was his way of having one last dance together, a way of saying goodbye to her, with the memory of a dance never forgotten.

Just before Sandy's death, we received news that my other sister-in-law, Kelly, and her husband, John, were going to have a baby. Of all of Charlotte's daughters, Kelly had been the one closest to Sandy. As one of his primary card-playing partners, they used to tease each other constantly. He often joked about her social life, pretending to be a strict parent while she often answered with comments about his clothing, which was always a bit on the sloppy side. The timing of this news in the context of Sandy's illness was of great comfort to our family. He had always loved babies; you could always see a twinkle in his eye when he was around them. Now, where there had once only been the potential for an ending, there was the news of a beginning.

For us, the cycle of life would run full circle, and it was just before Kelly gave birth that one last goodbye would be said. It arrived in a dream Kelly had during the time she and John were thinking of names for the baby. In her dream, Sandy said to name the baby after him.

Given Sandy's easygoing relationship with Kelly when he had been alive, it didn't surprise me that he had one last moment of fun with her. A joke shared between friends, and a way of saying goodbye, in the land of dreams where those who have departed will always be close.

Ed Bonapartian lives in Albany, New York and delights in sharing dream awareness both at home and in the community. He is currently working on a manuscript exploring the link between dreams and 12-step recovery. Ed is also the author of The Stories of Our Lives, *which can be ordered online at*

REAL STORIES OF SPIRIT COMMUNICATION

http://www.booklocker.com/books/1462.html or from any major bookstore.

11. Amy's Last Words
Vicky DeCoster

"There's a reason for everything," Amy used to say to me. Many years later, her words of advice still echo in my mind. Amy was my friend, co-worker, and a beautiful woman who was murdered on August 27, 1993 at the age of 26.

Amy and I knew each other for five years before she died. The halls at our office used to ring with the sound of her laughter. When she smiled, it was contagious. Everyone was her friend, no matter his or her color, faults, or disabilities. She was one who easily forgave you for your mistakes, but was honest with her opinions.

Since we spent eight hours a day with each other, we shared a great deal. We discussed many different subjects in our five years of friendship, our heartaches and our dreams of someday marrying and having children. Amy hoped to share her future with a husband who supported and loved her. She wanted a simple life, one full of the love and laughter of children. Her blue eyes shone with excitement when she shared her dreams.

It was with a deep passion that she maintained close relationships. She made friends easily because she had the ornate ability to listen without judgment. It was impossible to have conversations with Amy without laughter intervening at some point. It was shortly after I met Amy that she lost her 2-year-old nephew to cerebral palsy. She had difficulty recovering from the shock and pain of losing someone so young. During a lengthy conversation one afternoon, we discussed our spirituality and our strong desire to feel God during such a tragic loss. Although she worried about her nephew's happiness, I had no doubt that Amy had derived much peace from prayer. She confided in me that she believed in Heaven, God, and angels, and was comforted in knowing that her nephew was with God.

> "Amy, what's it like up there?"

There was no warning of Amy's death, except for the strong premonition I'd had the night before hearing of the murder. While standing in my laundry room, a feeling of utter terror and dread passed through me. I just knew something bad had happened. The next morning, after it was announced on the radio that Amy had been murdered, I realized that her body had been found in the same hour that I'd had my premonition.

Amy died from a single gunshot wound to her face. Her death was an unnecessary twist of fate and I struggled with the senselessness of the situation. She was only a few years younger than me. Amy had so much left to experience, so many more people left to touch.

In the weeks following her death, I spent many sleepless nights thinking about my friendship with Amy, angrily trying to search for the reasons behind her tragic death, and wondering where she was and if she was happy.

As the days passed slowly, I completed the task of cleaning out her desk at the office. I discovered photographs of Amy and our coworkers at the office Christmas party. I also found the name and phone number of her murderer on a small, white scrap of paper. Every item I examined seemed to bring a deep ache in my soul. Finally, I packed up the boxes and a coworker delivered them to her grieving family.

A few days later, homicide detectives came to the office to interview me. I was one of the last people to spend time with Amy the day she died. We had lunch together a few hours before she was killed.

It took weeks before I could walk past her cubicle and look inside. I rerouted my steps away from the department where she had worked. One day, I forced myself to walk into her empty cubicle and sit down. I did not stay a long time, but long enough to discover the pang of loneliness that accompanies losing a close friend. Her desk was barren, except for a calendar on which the pages had never been turned from the day she died. The cube was hollow sounding, her nameplate gone.

Grief was not a familiar emotion to me, so I turned to God for healing. Although I felt comforted after praying, I still did not feel at peace. Now I understood Amy's

> *I learned that there are no rules when you mourn. And while you grieve, life seems to be unbalanced.*

feelings after her nephew's death. Accepting the circumstances surrounding her death seemed to be the most difficult task. I learned that there are no rules when you mourn. And while you grieve, life seems to be unbalanced. There are many questions, but not many answers.

Finally, an answer to my questions came one night while I slept. As I dreamed, Amy suddenly appeared. We were in a room furnished with nothing but two chairs. Although I felt apprehensive about seeing Amy again because of the brutality surrounding her death, she looked beautiful and peaceful.

We sat in the two chairs and I immediately started asking her questions. "Did you see how many people were at your funeral?"

She replied, "Yes, I did." I asked if she'd seen me at the funeral and she said, "Just a minute, they'll play it back for me." She looked off in the distance and said quietly, "Yes, I saw you." She stood up and hugged me, seeming to understand the pain I felt at her funeral.

Knowing she would not be staying with me long, I asked the question that had been burning in my heart. "Amy, what's it like up there?" She answered with a smile, "You'll see someday. It's the most beautiful place you've ever seen. It's home, home, home."

Amy disappeared and has never returned to my dreams since that night. After the dream, I sat up in bed, knowing that what I saw could not be labeled a dream but, instead, a message from

Heaven. I woke my husband, and he reassured me that what I saw in my dream was real. I cried for some time and then fell into a deep sleep. The next morning, as I awakened, I finally felt the peace I had been looking for since Amy died. I visited her grave for the first time since the funeral and silently thanked her for such a wonderful gift.

There is a reason for everything. I may never know the reason why Amy was taken from this life so quickly, but I do know that she came back in my dream to tell me a beautiful story that I passed on to my friends, coworkers, and Amy's family, and will someday pass on to my children.

When my children ask me why I believe in Heaven, God, and angels, I can honestly answer, "Because Amy told me so." Her words in my dream still provide me with comfort, and seeing her smile again provided me with an inner-peace that will never be replaced. The Bible says that a faithful friend is a sturdy shelter and that, in finding one, we find a treasure. Amy may not be with me here on earth, but every time I comfort a grieving soul on earth with Amy's story, I know our eternal friendship was a gift from God.

Vicky DeCoster has written essays and articles for Atlanta Singles, Metro Parents, Omaha Magazine, Her Magazine, Omaha World-Herald, Christian Singles, *and* SingleLife. *Her essay "The Best Part of the Day" was published in* The Don't Sweat Stories *(forward by Richard Carlson, Ph.D.). Vicky's book of humorous essays,* The Wacky World of Womanhood: Essays on Girlhood, Dating, Motherhood, and the Loss of Matching Underwear *is available at http://www.wackywomanhood.com.*

12. Mother's Message
Renie (Szilak) Burghardt

I don't know much about my real mother, Irenke Szilak Balazs (see photo 1 on page vi), only that she died at the age of 19, a few weeks after I was born. Her mother rarely talked about her to me because it hurt too much. She never got over losing her daughter. But I do know one thing for certain about my real mother. She loved my father deeply.

When I was a child, my father was the stranger who occasionally came to visit me at my grandparents' home where I lived. Of course, I knew he was my father, but he seemed so awkward and shy in my presence that he made me feel uncomfortable.

It was during the spring of 1944 when I last saw my father. He brought me a shiny, new red bike, and he took me for a ride on it. I was seven years old and loved the bike. But when my father asked me for a hug after our ride, I offered him a handshake instead.

"I know I'm almost a stranger to you, but you are my only child and I love you," my father told me that day. "I loved your mama, too, more than I can ever say. When the war ends, you and I will get to know each other better, I promise you that."

My father never got the chance to make good on his promise because fate intervened. All this took place in the Bacska region of Hungary where I lived in 1944, while my young father was in the army. The war he spoke of was World War II, of course, and Tito and his communist partisans were soon breathing down our necks. My grandfather decided to move us to safer surroundings soon afterward. There was no time to notify their son-in-law of our move. Besides, we weren't sure where we would end up.

Of course, so much happened in the next three years, among them the Soviet occupation of Hungary. When we finally

> "You must get in touch with your father."

managed to escape, we landed in a refugee camp in neighboring Austria. Finally, in 1951, our hopes for a better life became a reality when we were allowed to immigrate to the United States. After we boarded the old Navy ship, *The U.S.S. General Stewart*, in September of 1951, on our way to America, we watched from the deck as the ship pulled out of the Bremen Haven, Germany harbor.

"We will never see our old homeland again," my grandfather lamented sadly.

"But we're on our way to America, the land of new opportunity!" my grandma added. It was at that moment that I thought of my father and the promise he had made the last time I had seen him. Perhaps he hadn't even survived the war, I thought and, if he did survive, we had no idea where he was.

In America, life was busy and good. My grandparents went to work and I went to school. We never talked about my father, and I can't recall ever thinking about him. It was as if he had never existed.

In June of 1954, after I had not seen my father for 10 years, something intervened on his behalf. I had gone to bed, as usual, my mind filled with plans for the coming weekend. I was going to a dance and a special boy would also be at that dance. Sweet promise was in the air.

Suddenly, a vision appeared at the foot of my bed. It was a beautiful young woman with long, flowing blonde hair, wearing a sad expression on her strangely familiar, lovely face. I sat up and gazed at her, not at all frightened, for though I had never met her and didn't even have a picture of her, I knew who she was. She was my mother.

She said in a voice that was just above a whisper, "You must get in touch with your father. He is very worried about you because he doesn't know what has happened to you. He needs to know that you are alive and well so he can go on with his life in peace. You must do this very soon." Then, she was gone, vanished into the thin air she had come from.

I sat there on the bed and began to cry. I cried for never having known her, and I cried for my father and all the sadness and worry I had caused him. My grandmother must have heard me because she came into my room to ask what was wrong. I told her about the vision. Or had it been a dream? I wasn't quite sure. Grandma began to cry, too, as I described the woman that had come to me with a message.

The following morning, my grandfather wrote a letter to some relatives who still lived in the old country, inquiring about my father. Three weeks later, I received a jubilant letter from him!

"Though we're separated by a great ocean now, I'm happy and relieved to know that you are alive and well, my dear child. Never forget that I will always love you. And I will always love your mama, too," my father wrote in that first letter. And when I answered his letter, I told him about the vision from my mother, and how she still loved him, too.

"I cried when I read your letter, my dear daughter. And oh how I wanted to visit the cemetery where your mother was laid to rest," my father then wrote. "However, the cemetery is long gone, having been plowed under by the communist regime. But I know that my darling Irenke knows that I will always love her, and one day she and I will be reunited in Heaven."

My father and I kept in touch over the years and even spoke by telephone several times but, unfortunately, we never had the chance to see each other again in person. And to this day, I regret not having given my father a hug the last time I saw him. When he finally went to his heavenly reward in 1987, my only consolation was that he and my mother were together again at last.

My grandfather passed away in 1965, and, in 1983 when I left the city behind and moved to a rural area, I brought my

> *"When you get home, look for my old prayer book hidden in one of my drawers. There is something in the prayer book that I meant to give you years ago."*

grandmother with me. She was 83 years old by then and still in fairly good health. But in 1985, she fell and broke her hip and, after that, her health deteriorated. She had a stroke and gangrene developed in one of her legs. The leg had to be amputated. Her mind became fuzzy due to hardening of the arteries and she had to be put in a nursing facility. Although she always knew who I was when I visited, she didn't exactly know where she was or what was happening to her.

When my grandmother was 89 years old, she landed in the hospital with pneumonia. I was very worried as I rushed to her side but, upon entering her room, I was surprised to find her sitting up, smiling, and more clear-minded than she had been in four years. We talked about my kids, her dear great-grandchildren, and about things I thought she had long forgotten. Then, as I was ready to leave with the thought of coming back the following morning, my grandmother suddenly said, "I have always done my best for you. I have loved you as my own child and my Irenke knows that. But before you leave now, I want you to know something. You are so much like your dear mother, so very much. She loved nature, too, and animals. Every spring, she waited for the return of our resident storks and would walk to the marsh to watch them catch frogs to eat. When you get home, look for my old prayer book hidden in one of my drawers. There is something in the prayer book that I meant to give you years ago. It is something your mother has left for you," she added, tears streaming down her face.

I hugged and comforted her by telling her how much I loved her and, when I was finally leaving, with the intention of returning the following morning, my grandmother waved and smiled at me. She looked so frail, but seemed so alert and happy that I was convinced she was going to make it after all.

When I got home, I immediately looked for the old, Hungarian prayer book. As I sat on the bed and opened its tattered pages with trembling hands, I found a small picture of my real mother. And then, I unfolded a little piece of paper and, to my surprise, found that it had a very faded poem written on it, a poem that was dated just two days before she died, dedicated to her baby girl, me. I sat there for a long time and, for the first time in my life, cried over the mother I never knew.

Then, picking up the slip of paper with the faded poem again, I suddenly found, to my astonishment, that it was no longer faded at all; it looked like it had just been written. The words of the poem positively glowed! I sat there holding that slip of paper, tears streaming down my face, until the phone rang.

"Your grandmother died peacefully in her sleep just a few minutes ago" a nurse from the hospital informed me gently.

"I know," I said quietly, "I know."

As she left her earthly home to join her loved ones in Heaven, my wonderful Anya left me with a most touching parting gift, making that night one of the saddest, yet most meaningful nights of my entire life. But I knew she and her Irenke were together at last.

Renie Burghardt, who was born in Hungary, is a freelance writer with numerous credits. Her writing has been published in magazines such as Angels on Earth, Mature Living, Midwest Living, Cat Fancy, Whispers from Heaven, *and others. She is a contributing writer to* Cup of Comfort, Cup of Comfort for Friends, Cup of Comfort for Women, Chicken Soup for the Christian Family Soul, *and* Chicken Soup for the Horse Lover's Soul, *and she has contributed to several* Chocolate for Women *books, the latest being* Chocolate for a Woman's Courage, *and* Chocolate for a Teen's Dreams. *Renie has also contributed to* God Allows U-Turns, The Big Book of Angels *(Rodale Press), several* Listening to the Animals *books (Guideposts), and many others. She lives in the country and loves nature, animals,* gardening, reading, writing, and spending time with family and friends. To get in touch with Renie, send an email to renie_burghardt@yahoo.com.

13. Culinary Cravings and A Broken Bucket
Kathleen Strattan

Being with my father during his illness, and when he died of cancer three years ago, was both deeply joyful and deeply sad and moving. I think we knew every bit of time we had with him was precious. Despite the grief and fear and difficulty facing death (he never stopped wanting to get well, and he didn't want to die), he never, up until the end, lost his wry, droll sense of humor, and his last words directed to me were ones of support and encouragement.

Although it seems almost universal to regret in hindsight things we did or didn't do for a dying loved one—and my mother and I have experienced our share of these regrets—one choice I have always been deeply glad we made during his last days was to bring him, no matter how much effort it took, whatever food he craved (soda, beer, ice cream, or coffee at 3 a.m.). It was a lot of trouble making trips to the nearest store when we lived way out in the country, and making coffee in the middle of the night when we were exhausted from round-the-clock care giving. But, looking back, my heart would break all over again to think we didn't give that precious person those last little bits of gratification and happiness, and I'm glad we didn't somehow talk ourselves out of bringing him the treats he craved. He was so pleased with that last cup of coffee in the wee hours of the morning, even though he could only drink a sip or two.

After his death, I longed for a sign that his soul somehow went on and didn't just come to an end. I remember sending out the prayer that he would send a double rainbow right away to let me know he was all right. That never happened.

What did happen could understandably be considered coincidence or could be attributed to some kind of heretofore-

> *It made me wonder how common this sort of thing really is.*

latent psychic ability on my part, although this definitely hasn't been a typical experience for me, before or since. So, for me at least, it's unusual. I was interested to discover that when I mentioned these seemingly coincidental events to others (actually, two women, a neighbor, and a cousin, each of whom had also recently lost their fathers), they weren't the least bit surprised and, in fact, relayed similar experiences to me. It made me wonder how common this sort of thing really is. This is nothing extreme, but here is my experience.

In the days and weeks right after my father's passing, I seemed repeatedly to be given, unknowingly by someone (a friend of my mother's, a neighbor, family members) the exact desserts I was craving at any particular time. This happened a lot during the first few weeks following my father's death. Whenever I felt like a certain sweet, no matter how obscure, it always seemed to materialize within the next 24 hours. And it wasn't like a lot of other desserts were arriving at the same time. These were the only ones. It's not like we're a family that's constantly being deluged by a smorgasbord of desserts!

If I felt like chocolate cake, someone would appear with chocolate cake. This was the first instance, and I believe this happened within 24 hours following my father's death. To my astonishment, my mother's friend appeared with not just a piece of cake, which would have been plenty, but an entire chocolate cake with peanut butter icing. These wishes often seemed to be granted with especial bounty and generosity. The quantity seemed to often be almost humorously greater than what I'd imagined.

When I felt like watermelon, the neighbors just happened to drop off some watermelon that day, left over from their cookout, wondering if we could use it. One time I'd been wishing for

Pepperidge Farm® chocolate chip cookies (a treat I have probably less than once a year) and my mother came home from a meeting bearing bags and bags of Pepperidge Farm® cookies that had been left over from a meeting and sent home with her! That same evening, my husband brought home a bag of even *better* homemade chocolate chip cookies his parents had sent with him, very much like the Pepperidge Farm® ones in appearance and texture, but with that added gourmet/homemade quality!

> *I would have felt sheepish mentioning this to many people...*

This seemed like something most other people would consider so trivial, despite the impression it made on me, that I mentioned it to very few people.

But for me, what happened last summer, two years after his passing, was the most striking incident yet. Again, I would have felt sheepish mentioning this to many people, although I did mention it to those few I felt might appreciate it.

We live on a "back-to-the-land" homestead with no running water, so that might give a little context to the problem we were having with our well, which is still the sole source of water for our two households here. (My husband and I are building our home on land next to my parents' homestead.)

Our cylindrical well bucket (called a West Virginia bucket) had come loose and fallen down the well. Mother and I were trying one thing after another to salvage that bucket from 90 to 100 feet below ground. First, we tried a hook on the end of a rope. No luck. Then we tried a strong magnet. No luck again. The magnet just stuck to the side of the metal pipe.

By the time we had finished these futile attempts, hours had passed. Mother and I were lamenting that we didn't remember how Daddy had "rescued" the bucket before (vaguely remembering this same thing happening sometime within the past 10 years). He would have thrived on helping us and solving the problem, while he was still living. Left to fend for ourselves, this lost bucket was a real challenge.

Mother said, "Maybe he'd have it in his files."

I went into his workshop to look. For months following my father's passing, I felt a sense of reverence when I went in there. This was his sanctuary, where he spent most of his time in life and where he did most of his woodworking and repair work.

He had accumulated four drawers of index cards arranged alphabetically, which was his system of note taking. When he wanted to go back and look up a procedure he had learned previously, he'd just look it up in his index card file.

I looked under "well," and there were about five "well" cards, even several about the West Virginia bucket. But I couldn't find anything about how to rescue it from the bottom of the well! There was one card describing how he'd fixed a leaky West Virginia bucket. He wrote about how he'd been stymied about it, but had prayed about it and right away, after that, the answer had come to him. The card went on to state that this prayer worked, and that he'd gotten the bucket fixed.

So, in that spirit, I prayed, too, hoping my father's spirit might help us find the answer for hauling that bucket up from the bottom of the well.

I opened the drawer where his journal/notebooks are kept on the off chance I could find the description of how he'd rescued the fallen bucket. It was my last hope, since there was nothing about it in the index cards.

He must have a hundred journals, little brown "pocket books" arranged chronologically. He was always a chronicler of events, ideas, and discoveries, but I had no memory of exactly what year it was that the bucket was last lost off the rope down the well, so I had no idea where to begin looking. It could have been any time from 1990 to 1999, probably some time in the middle. Looking through 10 years of those journals (without knowing the specific year the West Virginia bucket had last fallen down the well) would very likely take hours or days, and he might or might not have recorded this bucket-retrieving event in a notebook.

I picked up the closest pack of notebooks. The first one was blank; the second one was for some reason from 1997. It was obviously misfiled because it was dated three years before my father's death. While it seemed strange that this one from 1997 was in the top pack, I went ahead and started there.

Well, on about the third full page of *that* notebook, there it was! The entry was titled "caught a big fish today." He went on to describe how we had rigged up a system of five hooks to catch the West Virginia bucket and draw it up.

Five hooks! One hook might not catch the bucket handle, but one of five hooks, sticking out every which way, would have a better chance of catching it. We found the hooks, lowered them down the well, and when we pulled on it the second time, we caught the bucket!

These are probably modest examples compared with what others might have experienced in regard to communications from those who have passed on, but I marveled at them at the time they occurred, and I still do when remembering. Writing this, tears came to my eyes.

Kathleen Strattan lives in Narvon, Pennsylvania.

14. I Love You — I Always Will
Spider

It was another time—the summer of 1969. It was another place—St. Louis. It was another world—Vietnam threatened the young. They sought a new lifestyle that was better. Some found it in Love. I found it and lost it. But for you to understand it, I need to tell you a bit about the time and the lifestyle where it happened.

The Underground flourished. It was a time of Free Love freely given, of prayerful Peace being hoped for and achieved in small communes, and of drugs used for pleasure and escape: to search the mind and soul in hopes of finding the world we all wished to find. Yes, it was naive, simplistic, and doomed, but we didn't know it. We knew the Hippies would rule the world.

I was a part of all that. I was half owner of one of the more successful "head shops" in the city. We carried pipes, rolling papers, posters, glassware, beads, leather clothing, sandals, roach clips, and incense—anything that added to the "Hippie experience."

Before I was a Hippie and a Flower Child, I was in the Army. I did my time and, after discharge, went to college. I found myself with some people who founded a group that became known as The SORRATs. The SORRATs were founded to explore the mysteries of the mind, dreams, and all the other things that were unexplained. Parapsychology was just being explored and Dr. Rhine's studies and experimentation were adding credence to the subject. I knew quite a bit about PSI Studies, but was not yet ready to form an opinion as to the "Afterlife." Frankly, I had too much "Nowlife" to lead first.

It was 1969, and it was a good year. My partner and I had done well and had regular ads in the Outlaw, the local Underground newspaper, and on the two Underground FM radio stations.

The results were that we had a lot of people stopping by to sell us products.

A saleslady carrying an extensive line of stuff stopped by and was shown to the back office where Willie, my partner, and I were going over some bit of business. Clara, the saleslady, had her roommate with her to help carry the heavy sample cases. Her name was Bits.

Bits was a tiny thing, being barely five feet. She had sun-streaked hair of a light brown. Her eyes were dark brown and her lips were full and pouty. I was totally stricken by this beautiful elfin creature.

She nodded on being introduced to Willie and reached to shake my hand. Her fingers, like her hand, were small and gracefully slim. When we touched, it was as if I had been shocked, but pleasantly. Her eyes met mine. Something had happened. She laughed nervously and it was like bells tinkling.

It was hot, so we got some sodas for the girls and small-talked about head shop business while they cooled off. While talking about concerts and music, it was mentioned that Ted Nugent and the Amboy Dukes were doing a concert across the river (Missouri) in St. Charles that night. Our shop was a ticket outlet, so we had good seats. It was decided to have Willie and I take our cars and the girls would ride with us. That way, I could tend to the deposits and the other "Friday" things and meet them at the concert. The girls could leave their samples in the office and we would look them over and make an order the next day.

I opened the door to my Pontiac ragtop and let Bits in. She bounced over and unlocked my door. I had wondered if she would be a DDH (Damn Door Hugger), but she snuggled up to me like we had been together for years. The stereo was on one of the Underground stations and playing some good sets. I was in Heaven and off to a great concert with a truly beautiful girl at my side. We stopped at a light. Bits looked up at me and smiled a smile that captivated me completely. She thanked me for taking her to the concert. I think I just grinned a lot.

The concert was terrific. Nugent was a wild animal prowling the stage. The guitars screamed. Bits was on her feet half the time, dancing to the primitive beat. She made a lot of people enjoy the concert with her enthusiasm. All too soon, it was over.

We spent the night together. At first, I was nervous and wanted to be sure she had a good time. She bounced around and was totally natural, full of energy, and smiling that smile.

The next day was Saturday. We got the shop open after a good breakfast. That evening, we went to a bar we had some interest in. Bits danced all the slow dances with me. I'm not a good fast dancer at all, although I managed a couple to prove how bad I was. She laughed that musical laugh of hers, and tugged my beard so I would lean down and kiss her thoroughly. Someone called for a bucket of ice water to throw on us. The bar was happy. Bits was working her elfin magic.

The only dark point had happened earlier in the evening. I had taken Bits to eat (and to show off) at my favorite restaurant, Mama Rosa's. Mama Rosa was an Italian lady of extreme culinary skills who had "adopted" me. Bits and Rosa had instantly loved each other. At one point, Rosa had chided me about it "being time I got married and had some children." A dark expression of sadness and hurt had momentarily passed over Bits' lovely face. It was gone in an instant, but I had seen it. I was afraid to quiz her on it.

Sunday, I awoke to Bits making breakfast. The little mink could really cook. There were some parts of her that were definitely Southern. After breakfast, we went to Forest Park, the gathering place for all the Hippies. Bits delighted in the carnival atmosphere and made a lot of new friends. I was hard pressed to keep her in sight as she ran and played. At sundown, we went back to my place. I put on some music; we reheated the "doggy bags" from Rosa's, and cuddled on the couch for a long while.

The next day we went to the shop and Willie and I helped the girls get packed up so they could return to Kansas City.

Unfortunately (not really), Clara's old Chevy had a fatal engine noise. We wouldn't let the girls risk the highway with that. We contacted Stan's, a garage we often dealt with, and he agreed to hurry over. Fifteen minutes later, the tow truck pulled in and, surprisingly, the owner, Stan, was driving. He listened to the engine and pronounced it terminal. I looked at Willie and he nodded. We told Stan to tow it and fix whatever needed to be done. Clara protested that she couldn't pay for it, and I informed her that we would. Willie and I each got a very sincere kiss from the girls. We unloaded the girl's stuff, and I took Bits back to my apartment. Clara and Willie were going to do a tour of the other head shops in the city. That way, the trip would be profitable. I had Bits all to myself. I couldn't have been happier.

The next week was a blur of good meals and making love. It was a lot like a honeymoon.

I believe it was the fifth day when I woke up and Bits was sitting at the end of the bed just staring at me. I asked her if anything was wrong and she shook her head "No" and then "Yes." Her eyes were full of tears as she stammered something. I put my fingers to her lips to quiet her. This crying was the one emotion I never wanted to see her do. I kissed her and said, "Bits, I love you." It had come to me days before, but I had vowed not to say it unless the time was perfect for it. The tears were streaming down her cheeks as she snuffled back that she loved me, too.

I loved her and I wanted her in my life—she was my life. Nothing else mattered. She loved me! It was perfect. I didn't know what to do next. Bits was soon laughing and happy, and it seemed my beard got tugged for a kiss every five minutes the rest of the day. I really didn't mind.

Stan called and said the car was done all too soon. Reluctantly, I took Bits and her new bag (the old one couldn't handle all the new clothes I had bought for my elf) over to the garage to meet Clara.

Bits was subdued and very sad. If I hadn't had business interests to tend to, I would have driven her there and back.

She was going to put her affairs in order and would call me collect every night. As soon as everything was straight, she would come back and we would see what was going to happen with us.

I forced cheerfulness and tried not to notice how Bits clung just a little longer and kissed a little frantically before they pulled away. I had a sinking feeling in my stomach, and I felt sick and feverish. I was scared, and I didn't know why. I watched the old Chevy drive out of sight with foreboding.

It was the longest day I ever spent. Early evening, the phone rang and an operator asked if I would accept the charges. I didn't give her time to finish her little speech before I was yelling "Yes." It was Bits. They were safe!

Bits was crying and hiccupping and couldn't make much sense. God I missed her. She handed the phone to Clara who was puzzled. She didn't realize what had happened between Bits and me. We hadn't realized the depth of what had happened. Bits was sobbing in the background, and I was too choked up to talk. Willie gripped my shoulder for a moment to steady me, then took the receiver from my nerveless fingers. He and Clara talked for a few minutes. I could tell by the way Willie was talking that he and Clara were puzzled.

He handed the phone back to me. Bits had gained some control, although I could tell she was still crying. I couldn't think of anything to say. Bits choked out how she missed me—how she loved me. I told her I loved her and promised I was coming to see her. There wasn't much else to say.

Willie sat and talked to me nonstop for a half hour. It wasn't like him, but I guess he was worried and scared for me. I had never felt an emotion like this before. He finally told me that if I could hold out until Friday, he would take over and I could drive over to Kansas City for as long as I needed to. He hugged me and told me to hold on.

Tuesday, Wednesday, Thursday, Friday had never been so long coming before. Somehow I made it. The car was packed on Wednesday, repacked on Thursday, and I was on the road

When Loved Ones Return After Crossing Over

by 5:00 a.m. on Friday. The Pontiac never made a trip that fast anywhere in its life. I was on the outskirts of Kansas City in what must've been a new land speed record. I stopped at a pay phone and called to get directions. A sleepy Clara answered. I could hear Bits bouncing and squealing in the background. Clara gave me directions and, as I made the final turn, an elf exploded through the screen door and flew down the block. She half dove through the open window and I couldn't drive anymore with her in my arms. I got out of the car and carried Bits into the house as she frantically pulled my beard for the hungriest kisses I've ever had. Clara passed us as she went to move my car from the middle of the street. "Slick parking job," she muttered.

It was a glorious day! I felt better and Bits did, too. She kept saying "I love you" over and over like a mantra, as if I heard it enough, I would believe her. I knew I loved her more than ever. We came out of her room and sat with Clara in the living room for a while. By now, Clara was just amused by us.

As Bits was sitting on the couch with her legs tucked under her and I was on the floor, she was tangling her hand in my hair. I rolled up to one knee, took her slim hand in mine, and asked her to please marry me. I slid a ring on her finger that fortunately did fit. It was an engagement ring that one of my friends in the jewelry business had assured me was the best he had.

Bits froze—mouth hanging open and eyes wide. Clara gasped. Bits stared so long, I wondered if I had made a mistake. She finally swallowed hard and gasped out a squeaky "Yes." One "yes" wasn't enough for her—she kept saying it, "Yes, yes, yes, yes," as she dove on me from the couch and smothered me in kisses until I was gasping. I held her and promised to never let her go. She was quietly crying. Clara was crying, and I felt a need for a tissue, too.

The next two days went well, but all too soon it was time for me to get back to St. Louis. Bits couldn't come as she had a doctor's appointment she was waiting for. I told her I would come back and get her the weekend after next.

I drove back to St. Louis by myself. Clara, the big mouth, had called Willie and blabbed. He and a few friends were waiting for me. I got razzed, heckled, pummeled, and drunk. It was their way of congratulating me. Everything was great.

Bits was very lovey on the phone when I called her the next day. We had a nice talk and assured each other that we loved each other. The next couple of phone calls were similar. I won't go into detail as that much saccharin isn't good for anyone. We were as happy as we could be being apart. Bits' doctor appointment was the next day and I thought she sounded a bit reserved—even scared. I asked her why, but she wouldn't say.

I called the next day to see what was going on. Bits didn't much want to talk, but said she was going in for another test the next day. It didn't dawn on me that that was on a Saturday until later when I was worrying out loud to Willie. He pointed it out and seemed to think there was something odd.

I called the next day and got Clara after the third try as I was becoming frantic. She was concerned, as she had gone to meet Bits at the hospital where they were to do the test or whatever it was. Bits hadn't been there. She did show up a few minutes later. I was relieved and asked her what was wrong. She wasn't communicating and I was babbling. I kept telling her how wonderful it would be to finally get married and how I couldn't wait to have children. She got real silent. She said goodbye, as if I were a wrong number and then she hung up. I dialed back, but got no answer. I tried every half hour or less until I finally got Clara when she got back from the store. She couldn't find Bits. She stayed on the phone with me and questioned me as to what I had said. When I got to the part about the children she stopped me and asked, "Didn't she tell you? She had had a hysterectomy a few months ago."

I had seen the scar, but had assumed it was an appendectomy or something. No wonder she had acted funny when kids were mentioned at Mama Rosa's, and now by my big mouth. She couldn't have them. I was in for another shock—Clara said that Bits was only 19. There was a lot more history I knew nothing about concerning her childhood and abuse, physical, mental, and sexual from what Clara was saying. I knew too little about my love. I knew she had seemed to be the happiest person I had ever seen. God could she act. Inside she must be desperate. Clara promised to call if she heard anything.

> *I was so scared—more scared than when I was under fire in Vietnam.*

The next morning, Clara called and said she had called everywhere she could think of without results. She had called the doctor that Bits had seen and talked to his nurse. The nurse had been alarmed and had told Clara that she couldn't say what, but the test had not gone well, and she was concerned for Bits' safety. The doctor came on the line and said he was going to inform the police because Bits had seemed so depressed. He would get them to put out an All Points Bulletin. I told Clara I was going to pack and if she heard anything to call my apartment as I would be there. I'd get to Kansas City as soon as I could. She said to hold off until she knew more.

Days passed. I wandered around and picked stuff up and threw it down. How long did it take to find an elf? I was so scared—more scared than when I was under fire in Vietnam. I had never had anything scare me like this. I couldn't wait, but I had to. After an eternity, the phone rang.

It was Clara. She said, "It's not good. You need to sit down. The police found Bits at a motel south of my place. She checked in several nights ago. She took an overdose of something. I—I'm sorry, but she's dead."

I don't know if I hung up the phone or not. I just walked out and got in my car and drove to Kansas City. Somehow, I managed to find Clara's place. There was a police car out front. They took one look at me and took away my keys. I guess I

REAL STORIES OF SPIRIT COMMUNICATION

> *I looked down. It wasn't her. Not my Bits. It was a husk she used to be in, but it wasn't her.*

was a mess. It must've been shock. I still couldn't believe it. I stayed with Clara and slept on the couch. Neither of us went into Bits' room. I couldn't believe she was gone. I started crying in the middle of the night. I guess I kept getting louder and louder. I cursed God with all the hate I could muster, but I guess He knew the strain I was under. I wound up on the floor sobbing, with Clara holding me and crying, too.

For some reason, they did not perform a full autopsy on Bits and released her body after a few miserably long days. Clara and I had found a mortuary that would handle the details of her burial. Bits had no living family that Clara had ever heard of so there was only us. We found a church that would let us have a service. When the preacher heard of the circumstances, he contacted a member of his church who was a psychiatrist. He took a look at me and wrote a prescription. I felt a little better and didn't cry so much—for a while.

Willie showed up with my black suit. He and the other guys at the head shop and bar had sent flowers. There was a big wreath from Mama Rosa and her family. It seemed like everyone I knew was there. My landlady had even come. I didn't know who had driven her.

When it was time for the service, I was supposed to go up and see her in the casket. My legs were water. I couldn't stand. Willie helped me to walk. I stood there for a long time without looking down at her. I guess if I didn't look, I could pretend it wasn't her. I looked down. It wasn't her. Not my Bits. It was a husk she used to be in, but it wasn't her. She was free and not here! They told me later that I started crying and laughing all at the same time and yelling it wasn't her. I don't know. I passed out. I hadn't eaten for three days and I went into some kind of shock. I was sedated by a doctor I didn't know, and they drove me to the burial. I didn't know what was going on or I would've probably jumped in the grave.

When Loved Ones Return After Crossing Over

The next few days were a nightmare. I left cleaning out Bits' room to Clara. She told me later it was one of the hardest things she had ever done. It was like she was throwing away a friend. I told her I didn't want anything. What was in my mind was enough. Later, I would wish differently.

Someone took me back to St. Louis and brought my car. There was a letter waiting for me. It was from Bits. She said for me to remember she did truly love me. She said she was sorry we couldn't grow old together and have children like I wanted. She said she had had a hysterectomy and couldn't bear my children. She said that they had not gotten all of the cancer—it was back and growing rapidly. She asked me to forgive her for taking her life, but she was afraid of the pain. She said if she could, she would watch over me and be with me—somehow. She said she was mine and would wait until we could be together again. She asked me to not forget her. She would love me forever.

If I'd had a gun in the house, I would've joined her. I read the note until my tears made the ink run and it was a rag of pulp. In the bottom of the envelope was the ring I had given her. The pain was more than I could bear. They found me on the floor a day or so later suffering from severe alcohol poisoning. I was in the hospital for a while. Honestly, it was all a blur.

It took me a month to get on my feet again. Something was gone out of me, though. I just went through the motions. I had one thing left to do. I drove to Kansas City and went to Clara's house. Some lady with too many kids lived there now. I called on her phone to find out from Clara's boss where she had moved. He said she had quit and left town. No one knew where. I thanked the lady and left a hundred dollars under the phone. It wasn't the same house anymore, and for that I was grateful.

I found the mortuary and they told me how to find Bits' grave. I went there. Good old Willie had bought a marker for that small grave. On it was her last name, which I hadn't

REAL STORIES OF SPIRIT COMMUNICATION

The TV went off. I checked and it was unplugged.

remembered, and her birth date, which I didn't know. I knelt there for a while letting the pain wash over me. I dug down in the loose earth and left her ring with her. I walked away and never went back. My Bits wasn't there.

Life was up and down. I got to where I couldn't stand St. Louis. Willie reminded me of what I had lost. I didn't dare drink, so I started on drugs. They didn't work either. I latched onto a beautiful nurse who was looking for an adventure. She had long, fiery red hair. We ran away to Arizona, but I guess that wasn't far enough. She and I drifted apart. She went to St. Louis for a visit and never came back. I was doing artwork from a studio I had at my apartment. It was all pretty stupid and mindless.

So life went for several years. I lived alone except for my cats. One in particular was the leader, Yeller. He was special, having been born on July 4th the year after Bits died. I had gotten used to not having company. I was miserably lonely and unhappy.

One night, I was feeling sad for some reason I couldn't understand. I had been depressed all day and yet felt like something was going to happen. Yeller was with me on my couch, watching television. A breeze stirred the curtains. I got up and checked the windows. I had the air conditioning on and no windows were even cracked open. I sat back down. The TV went off. I checked and it was unplugged. I didn't know how, but I figured it was a cat. However, they were all in the bedroom cowering except for Yeller, who was with me. The breeze blew the gauzy curtains again. They seemed to have a shape in them. The hair on my neck started crawling. I walked over to the curtains and heard a sound like laughter. It was familiar.

Yeller was all frizzed up and staring at the curtains. I didn't move a muscle. I just stared, trying to see. I heard the laughter again. It was a woman's laugh—like bells tinkling. The curtains stirred and a small woman's shape seemed to be forming in them. I hoped I knew who it was. I walked to the curtains and stood there. The laughter was coming from there. Something tugged my beard and as I moved with it, I felt the brush of lips on mine. I was so startled I fell on my butt right there. I felt a form fit into my lap as I sat there. Again my beard was tugged and, this time, there was a definite pressure on my lips. I could feel a woman's body pressed against mine. It lasted only a few seconds and was gone. In my mind, a voice seemed to say, "I love you—I always will."

You may doubt me if you wish. I only know that she said she would find a way and I think she might have. The date was July 30, 1974. Bits was buried on July 30, 1969. Exactly five years.

Since then, I have had periodic dreams of those 10+ days when I was the happiest man in the world. I talk to Bits a lot, as I get older. All the people who were in my life back then are long gone. No one is left to remind me, yet I believe she is waiting for me. We will be together again somehow. We have to be! Bits—I still love you, too.

Named "The Most Outstanding Artist of the Decade" by the readers of Impressions, *a magazine devoted to t-shirt decoration, Spider designed t-shirts for over 40 years. A Missouri native, Spider later found himself in the deserts of Arizona. Being unable to do art after a debilitating stroke, he started writing again. Spider has written hundreds of articles and four books on the technical side of screen-printing. Far from being retired, he claims to be ready for another 50 years or so, "if you'll read my stuff."*

15. We Are All Eternal Beings
Peggy Feldkamp-Allen

Vesta Crabtree passed away after a long bout with pancreatic cancer in 1978. She was buried in Ashland Alabama on Mother's Day. We called her "Bubbie" (see photo 10 on page vi). She was my grandmother.

Born on March 8th, 1900, my Bubbie saw the birth of the technological America. She experienced prohibition and saw the production of the first automobiles, telephones, radio, and television. She was a modern woman of her time. She drove her own car, smoked cigarettes, and became part of the women voters of America. After being widowed in 1935, she became a bootlegger in rural Clay County, Alabama as a means to support her three sons. She went on to open the first School of Beauty in Columbus, Georgia. Then she watched her sons leave first for World War II and then for the Korean War. In her lifetime, she saw World War I, World War II, the Korean War, the Cold War, the Cuban Missile Crisis, and the Vietnam War. Bubbie was a very strong and loveable soul. She lived her life as a single and independent woman at a time when it just wasn't done. And she made it.

Everyone loved Bubbie. She was 5 feet 9 and had auburn hair and hazel green eyes. She fancied herself as a "not too shabby" look-alike for Claudette Colbert. And she was, only prettier. Bubbie was a bright and bubbly person with a wonderful sense of humor. The room seemed to light up when she entered it, and the party began. She loved to dance. In her youth, all of her friends and family came to Vesta's house to have a good time. That continued until she became ill.

During Bubbie's illness, she came to live at home with us. My father was her youngest son. At the time, we lived in Alexander City, Alabama. So Bubbie had to give up her independence and her apartment in Ashland for the first time since 1935. She said the hardest thing she could remember having to do was to depend on someone else.

> She looked up into my face with tears in her eyes and said, "I am afraid."

As her condition progressed, eating became difficult and painful. Shortly before she had to be hospitalized, my father was preparing her meals. On this particular day, he had tried everything; soup, salad, sandwiches, soft eggs—you name it, he tried it. But she just couldn't eat anything. He became exasperated and swore. I still laugh remembering Bubbie sitting in the kitchen at the table. She turned around to face him, draping her arm over the back of her chair and, with a glint of humor in her eye, she told him "When I'm gone, I'm gonna come back and haunt you." At the time, we all laughed. Of course, at the time, none of us thought a thing about the remark as anything other than a joke.

The week Bubbie passed, I had sensed she was leaving us soon. My father, an insurance salesman, was on the road. Bubbie was to be hospitalized the following day. The night before, I went in her room to kiss her goodnight. She was lubricating her tongue because she didn't have any saliva, a common side effect of pancreatic cancer. She looked up into my face with tears in her eyes and said, "I am afraid." I asked her why. She said, "Because I know I am dying." We talked about our religious beliefs and I added, "Then don't be afraid. You will close your eyes in this world, and you will open them and be with Jesus. Your body is dying, not you. The person that looks out of your eyes is you, your soul, not your body. That spirit, that person that you are, cannot die."

Bubbie answered, "I guess you're right. I've never thought of it that way."

I then told my Bubbie, "Remember, when you get there, God promises the desires of your heart, so if you want to see us, you can." I kissed my Bubbie goodnight and, the next day, we

> "Remember, when you get there, God promises the desires of your heart, so if you want to see us, you can."

had to put her in the hospital. A few days later, she passed, but not before my father arrived. It seemed as though she waited for him. That was May of 1978.

In 1979, my father began seeing something late in the evenings while watching the Johnny Carson Show. Then he began hearing his name called. Soon after, my brother began hearing someone calling his nickname. The only person who ever called him "Clayboy" was Bubbie. It took about a year for the two of them to tell the rest of us because they were afraid we would think they were nuts. They didn't even tell each other. Finally, in 1980, my father told my mother by way of asking her if she had seen anything strange or heard voices in the house. My mother broke out in laughter. It seems she had been aware all along and kept it to herself. She felt her presence like an aura of warmth that made her feel bubbly whenever Bubbie was present. Upon hearing this, my brother confessed his secret, too.

One of the funny things about Bubbie visiting us was that every time my father saw her, which was frequently and always during Johnny Carson, he fell to his knees and turned white. That tickled my mother to tears. Once my sister saw her and ran screaming from the house in the middle of the day. The neighbors called the police because they thought she was being attacked.

It was January of 1980 when I returned home to my parents and I began seeing the apparition of my Bubbie and hearing her voice as well. But, in the beginning I thought it was my mother that I was seeing and hearing. While watching the George and Gracie Show, I saw what appeared to be a woman with short, dark, curly hair in a blue quilted robe come out of my mother's bedroom and go into the bathroom, but leaving the door cracked open. Then I would hear my name called, "Peg, Peg." Only my Bubbie called me Peg. I would get up and go into my mother's room and find her in bed reading a book. I would ask her if that had been her and she would answer that she hadn't been out of bed. Then she would laugh. At first, this fried my nerves and I began pulling the covers over my head each night I saw this apparition and heard my name called.

Then one night, something different happened. I saw her again, only this time, she went into my daughter's bedroom. I got up and looked inside to see someone whom I thought was my mother tucking my daughter's covers in around her. I went back to the living room and she went into the bathroom leaving the door ajar and called my name. I waited until the show I was watching was over, which was 11:30 p.m. that night. I then went to my mother's room and asked her if my daughter had kicked her covers off. My mother responded by asking, "I don't know, you better check and see." I looked at her as though she was crazy and she began laughing. At first, I thought she was playing a prank, but she told me to sit down. You see, my face had gone stark white.

Mother began explaining to me the previous events my father and brother had experienced and the feelings of happiness and warmth she had experienced. She went on to tell me that it could only be Bubbie because the blue quilted robe was what she had been sent to the funeral home in, and it was never returned.

She said, "She promised she would haunt us, didn't she? And she is." She laughed and said she thought it was delightful; especially that she left the door ajar for light. My daughter was afraid of the dark and, to help break that habit, my mother and I never indulged her complaint. Mother explained that the apparitions only seem to appear around the holidays and during times when serious family events occurred such as me coming home with my child, my brother's injury on the job the previous year, which brought him home, and the deaths of Bubbie's remaining sisters.

I couldn't quite grasp it at first. I had actually seen my Bubbie tuck in my baby and kiss her. I then knew that was what I'd seen. Only Bubbie tucked the covers in and folded them down at our neck.

The occurrences began to increase, probably because we were all in the house together again. In the beginning, my father had only seen the wisp of the apparition floating fast through the living room and heard his name called. Then one night, while watching Johnny Carson, he saw her more clearly. None of us could ever quite make out the face but, this time, my father could see the hair and the blue quilted robe. She moved very fast from the hallway through the living room to the front door. The front door opened and slammed so hard it shook the windows.

My father got up and went to the front door. At the same time, my mother got up and came out to see who had come in the door. The door was bolt locked. My father fell to his knees and had a slight stroke. His face was white and he looked sick. He didn't like talking about this.

My father was uncomfortable with these visitations because he was suffering from guilt. When Bubbie passed, we didn't know until the autopsy that she had pancreatic cancer. The doctor had misdiagnosed her condition as an addiction to pain medications. So, all pain medication was removed from her. Therefore, she suffered in great pain the last month of her life. My father felt guilty over this and thought that the haunting was a punishment.

Soon after my father's stroke, I moved my family to Cullman. But shortly before we moved, we got a message from Bubbie. There was a heater grate in the hallway floor that we kept covered during the summer with a rug. It was rubber backed and approximately 1½ to 2 inches thick. My bedroom door could not be closed over it. You had to remove the rug in order to close or open my door. One day, in broad daylight, the door was slammed across the rug, hitting the doorframe so hard it

When Loved Ones Return After Crossing Over

bounced back across the rug and left a doorknob impression in the plaster. It was done with such force that we thought a car had struck the house. I suppose Bubbie did not want us to move. But in 1988, we moved anyway. Turns out, in the end, she was right. We should not have moved.

> Most people would think my story is crazy.

The visitations did not occur in Cullman. I only stayed a year and a half. The area was infected with satanic worship. During that time, my father left his faith, or had already lost it, and left my mother for another woman. My mother ended up coming back to Auburn with me in 1993.

Shortly thereafter, the visitations began again. This time, they were more visible. To me, it was as though she was trying to tell us we did the right thing coming back. She would peak her head around corners. You could just make out a smiling face and then she would be gone.

Since then, my Bubbie has been with me a lot. One occasion occurred as I was walking though an upstairs bedroom. My daughter collected racecar soda cans. One flew off the dresser and across the room, and rolled on the carpet right up behind my heel, but did not hit me. I laughed all the way downstairs.

There have been many times that Bubbie has let me know she was there, especially times when I was alone, lonely, or sad. Her presence helped me persevere.

Now my uncle lives with me. He is my Bubbie's oldest son and is 84 years old. One spring day, my mother and I and my uncle were at the back door. My mother had just closed the back door and secured it for the evening. My uncle had turned to walk into the kitchen. I was behind him and my mother was behind me. We hadn't passed completely from the utility room into the kitchen when the back door opened all the way and slammed shut. Mother had locked the door. We all stopped in our tracks and began to laugh. Then we all said, "Hello, Bubbie."

My Bubbie's most recent visit occurred on my daughter's birthday, July 1st, at 4:30 a.m. Everyone in the house was sound asleep except me. I have chronic insomnia. I was watching a Hepburn-Tracey movie when my bedroom door opened all the way and then slowly closed all the way. There is duct tape on my door jam and the door mechanism because it is broken. You cannot open my door so quietly. You have to shove it open. The significance of this for me was comfort from Bubbie. You see, my daughter wasn't speaking to me or allowing me to see my only grandchild and I had been praying about that. So, Bubbie came on her birthday and gave me a spiritual hug.

Most people would think my story is crazy. We usually only tell it to Christian believers. If your faith is as strong as a mustard seed, it can move mountains. We wanted her with us, and she must have desired it, too, because God has allowed it. Partly, I know some of the reason why.

When I was 15, my Bubbie looked me in the face and told me that my life would be suffering, that I would not find happiness in this world. At the time, I didn't have a clue what she meant. Today, I am 46 years old. There aren't words enough to describe the life I have led and the cards that were dealt to me. But Bubbie has been with me. That has helped sustain me and keep my faith strong. Otherwise, I should probably not be here today sharing my faith with you.

We are all eternal beings. Only our bodies die. When God created us in His own image, He wasn't speaking of the physical fleshly body. That was given to us for our pleasure. God was referring to the Spirit. The Soul is the image of God. It is eternal. It cannot die.

Peggy Feldkamp-Allen was born in Richmond, Virginia. She is a single, 46-year-old mother and grandmother. Writing is her passion and she has been writing since the age of 10. Most of her inspiration for her work comes from life experiences. She has recently published a book of poetry, Poetry from the Soul, *on lulu.com. She believes that a person's best work comes from what life teaches us. Her deepest feelings and thoughts are expressed through her poetry. She has published magazine articles online worldwide and has three nonfiction works in progress;* Silent Screams, Death In Montezuma, *and* Evil Wore a Smile. *She has published her poems in anthologies worldwide and holds a membership in the National Institute of Writers. She also writes for others. If you would like your story told, you can contact her at pfeldkampallen@yahoo.com. Peggy is a born again Christian who practices the nondenominational messianic Christian faith. She believes the Bible as translated in the King James Version. Currently, she resides in a rural area in Alabama where she cares for her mother and stepfather.*

16. I'm Okay!
Peggy Feldkamp-Allen

It was the year 1970. Kendra and I met in junior high school in Jacksonville, Florida. We were both in the seventh grade. At first, we didn't like each other. Isn't that always the way of it with children? Opposites do attract. Kendra was a slim and trim redhead with big brown eyes and I was auburn haired with hazel green eyes and slightly chubby. We met in the girl's bathroom. I was just about to exit when Kendra came in. She spoke to me and said, "Hey girl, I hear you're a real bitch." I laughed, and remarked, "Well, I hear you're a real slut." Kendra laughed and, from that moment on, we were friends. Over the next few years, we became inseparable.

Kendra's father, Bruce, was an architect. His hobby was hydroplane boat racing. He raced all over the state of Florida in amateur and pro-am hydroplane boat racing events. Kendra, her sister, Jenny, myself, and a couple of girlfriends comprised his all-girl pit crew. He even had t-shirts made for us.

A race was coming up in Frostproof, Florida. For reasons beyond my understanding, my father would not permit me to go. It was the one and only time he refused to allow me to go anywhere with Kendra. I would soon discover why. My father had premonitions, which he usually kept to himself until they came true.

That weekend, Kendra's father was killed during the race, right before her eyes at Frostproof, Florida. His boat hit a still spot in the water and took a nosedive, breaking the boat in half. His neck was broken and he died instantly. My father knew something would happen that weekend but he didn't share that information. Unbeknown to us, Kendra's mother, Lucy, had experienced a similar feeling.

Lucy recounted the events of that weekend to me after it was all over with. She told me that upon seeing the accident, she saw her husband give the all-clear sign. They had agreed that should he ever have a mishap, if he was okay, he would raise his arms above his head and crisscross wave them to let her know he was okay. Lucy saw him make the sign. When the rescue workers and police got to Kendra, she was hysterical. Then Lucy got to her and told everyone it was all right, that her father had given the all-clear sign. The rescue workers and police thought she was in shock because they knew he was dead. His body was being loaded into the ambulance. This was very traumatic for Kendra because she was first told by rescuers that her father was killed, then her mother told her he was okay, and then she saw his dead body being taken away. She went into shock.

After the funeral, Lucy reflected back on what she had seen and shared with us that she believed Bruce was letting her know that everything would be okay. Bruce had foresight. He had provided for his family in the event of his death. Lucy was intuitive. She could sometimes sense things before they happened. She could sometimes tell a person what they were thinking or about to say and she could sometimes predict things that hadn't happened yet. Most people regard this type of thing as nonsense and I was one of those people until I experienced it firsthand through my association with their family. Over the years, I had become a part of the family. There were many times when Lucy told me things that came true. She also had a knack for catching Kendra and I at our shenanigans. Even when we were not where we were supposed to be, we were caught. It didn't take me long to realize you couldn't put anything over on Lucy. Although she did not sense Bruce's death, she had been apprehensive about the race. Before the race, an owl had gotten into the garage. To Lucy, this was a bad omen, which meant there would be a death.

A few months after Bruce's death, Lucy and the girls began seeing him in parts of the house, mostly in the master bedroom. The sightings were so frequent that Lucy moved out of the room and gave it to Julie. Julie saw him in the shower

> *I screamed like a banshee and went running out of the shower...*

and traded rooms with Kendra. Kendra never vocalized whether or not she saw him, but being that she was "Daddy's girl," I don't think it would have frightened her. I always believed Kendra was comforted by his presence. After a couple of years, Lucy had remarried.

By the time Kendra and I were 20 years old, Lucy and her new husband had moved out of the house into an apartment and given the house to us girls to live in together. The reason was that Lucy was no longer comfortable with the presence of Bruce in her new marriage. I moved in with Kendra and Julie. They had neglected to tell me about Bruce's frequent visits, probably because they were afraid I wouldn't move in. However, not lacking a sense of humor, they honored me with the master bedroom.

The first week in residence, I was taking a shower in the master bath. I had my hair lathered up with shampoo and turned my back to the shower nozzle to rinse. Upon opening my eyes, there stood Bruce in the corner of the shower staring at me. I screamed like a banshee and went running out of the shower, naked, covered with shampoo lather, into the hallway screaming for Kendra. Julie fell down laughing because she knew what had happened. Kendra came running into the hall to see what was going on, took one look at me, and broke out laughing until she cried.

After getting myself rinsed, dried, and dressed, we all sat down in the living room and Julie and Kendra began telling me the story explaining that their father's visits were the reason Lucy had moved out. Since it didn't bother Kendra and Julie, it made good sense for them to live there being that the mortgage was so small and that it was their childhood home. We had a good laugh. Lucy came over and explained to me that she felt Bruce was simply watching his girls grow up. Nonetheless, I moved into the bedroom at the other end of the house that had been converted from a garage.

I lived with Kendra and Julie for a couple of years until each of us married and moved on with our lives. During our time together, we enjoyed our "practical joke," which we played on many an overnight visitor. Many of our friends showered in the master bath and met Bruce. And to our delight, they reacted much the same as I did on my first meeting with Bruce as a spirit.

The house was eventually sold as we girls moved on in our lives. We don't know if Bruce remained with the house or moved on himself, but none of use will ever forget our youth spent in Jacksonville, Florida where we experienced puberty, first love, death and loss, and spiritual visits by Bruce, former amateur hydroplane boat racer. I, personally, always believed that Bruce stuck around because losing him hit Kendra so hard. I think his presence pulled her back into living and relishing her life. Kendra, Julie, and I have been friends now for over 30 years. We love each other very much. I dedicate this story to Kendra, Julie, and Lucy because they brought so much love and happiness into my life.

Peggy Feldkamp-Allen's bio appears in the preceding chapter.

17. A Father's Love
Heide AW Kaminski

In 1959, a little girl was born. Her parents were not married and, in those days, pregnancy outside of marriage was a horrendous thing. So the existence of the little girl was hidden from as many people as possible. Being so young, she was unaware of her circumstances.
One day, during her third year in this world, her parents decided it was time to put an end to the secrecy. The little girl had her judgment day. Her mother's sister organized a spectacular Catholic wedding for her respectable daughter.
Unaware of her impending "trial," the little girl happily skipped along a hallway holding on to her daddy's hand. "They are just going to love you!" he assured her over and over. That little girl was I (see photo 7 on page vi and photo 34 on page viii).
I do not remember my childhood. My brain has forever closed the doors to the memories. I can only recall glimpses and most of them take on the form of angry monsters. There are so many pieces to the puzzle of my life, and so many more are missing. Those, which appear on the draft table, are insufficient to create a picture. Fragments of my memory are forever buried in the backyard of my childhood.

My judgment day must have not gone over the way my daddy (see photo 35 on page viii) imagined it for I have been the "black sheep" of the family for most of my life. My parents split up when I was four. All I recall of the separation is the pain and loss I experienced. My daddy left me with the person who hated me the most—my mother.
I was a constant reminder of her unforgivable sin. And worse, I was a daddy's girl, through and through. I remember, from my teen years, a time when the memory blocking process gave way to rebelling and fighting against them rather than

forgetting them. On a daily basis, my mother spewed ugly words about my father. They were always followed by, "...and you are just like him!"

He died when I was eight years old. No one bothered to tell me. When I was old enough to figure it out, all that was left for me to say goodbye to was a brief visit with his weathered and unkempt grave. I often looked up to the skies and prayed for a sign from him. When I was in my 30s, I began exploring a broader range of spirituality than I had been exposed to before. I never felt quite at home with my mother's Atheism, my friends' Lutheranism and my first husband's Methodism.

Metaphysics gave me a path that felt right to me. I began consulting psychics. One particular medium came highly recommended by a friend. As it was quite a long way to travel, that friend came along for the ride. My friend made herself comfortable in an adjacent room, out of earshot, and she worked away on knitting a new sweater while I had my hour of enlightenment.

The psychic's husband was the only other person in the room where my reading took place. His presence was required to audiotape the session as his wife worked. She ended her fascinating reading with the statement "Do you have one question that remains unanswered?"

Without hesitation, I replied, "I always knew it in my heart, but I have to know for sure. Does my daddy love me?"

Immediately the medium's husband looked up and asked, "Who is here?"

My friend told me later that she froze in the midst of her knitting. Both had felt the presence of a very powerful energy. Myself, I sat "nailed" to my chair, gasping for air. I was enveloped by a tight grip that literally took my breath away. But instead of panic—which would seem to be a normal reaction to this sort of situation—the feeling of utter peace and love overcame me. I burst into tears.

"What happened?" asked the medium.

"He just hugged me!" I sobbed.

For many years thereafter, I did not hear from my father again. But my heart was at peace, for now I knew for sure that he loved me. For the little girl in me, hurting from a childhood full of "I hate you," this was all I needed to be happy.

A few years ago, I went to a spiritual workshop. While meditating, I saw a bright light. Cautiously I approached the light's center. My dad smiled at me and took my hand. Suddenly I was two years old again, skipping along the hall with him while he beamed over and over, "You are so adorable. Everyone is just going to love you!"

I have not heard from my father since. But that is okay. I know he is by my side—always; no matter what is going on in my life at any given moment. I never have to feel unloved again.

Heide AW Kaminski is a freelance writer based in Michigan. She has a children's book published in her native country, Germany, is a contributor to numerous anthologies, and author of Get Smart Through Art *(ISBN 0967088690), available at http://www.daycarerecordkeeping.com. She currently writes about interfaith issues on a regular basis for a monthly spiritual newsletter,* The Interfaith Inspirer, *and for a bi-monthly local newspaper,* The Good News, *covering community theater reviews, outstanding students in her community, charity events, and other positive happenings in her county. She also has an online monthly humor newsletter,* Sarcastic Women on the Loose, *and is looking for an agent/publisher for a paranormal romance novel she co-wrote with Dorothy Thompson and Pam Lawniczak. Heidi's personal website is http://www.thewriterslife.net/Kaminski.html.*
Her spiritual website is located at http://www.interfaithspirit.org/newsletter/articles.php.
Her newsletter can be found at http://www.topica.com/lists/SarcasticWomen.

18. Yappy
Steve Snider

Yappy (see photo 20 on page vi) is (was) a black cat, glossy, gleaming black. He was vain about it, too. I caught him pulling offending white hair out several times (while pretending that he was doing something else, like washing his immaculate coat).

Yappy was born in St. Louis and had an attitude born of that city, a kind of aloof arrogance and macho complex. I was living with a lovely girl, who would later become my wife. She was a redhead with a temper. I think that that was where Yappy learned to tease. Carol would scream at me, "Get your damn cat!" I'd go see and, sure enough, he would have committed some transgression just to get a rise out of her. It never failed. She did love him, too.

Our relationship with Yappy started when I was at home alone early in July. The windows were open for much needed air. I had a cobbled together fan I had salvaged and was trying to coax some more life out of it. A bunch of kids were walking down the alley, crying. I'm a sucker for crying kids and will do almost anything to restore peace and quiet. I asked them what the matter was.

The kids told me that they had to get rid of "this," a paper bag. I opened it and in the bottom was a mewling black kitten with its eyes still closed. It couldn't have been more than a week old. The kids said the kitten's mother had gotten out and was killed by a car. Their dad said they had to get rid of the last surviving kitten of her litter.

I looked at the kitten and softened. I told the kids I would take him. They made me promise I would take care of him. I promised a sacred oath and they skipped back the way they had come, happy now that the kitten had a home.

I needed to feed him and he looked like he had missed a few meals. I was raised on a farm and caring for orphaned animals was part of what you did. I called a vet and he gave me a recipe for formula I could make out of common grocery items to replace mothers milk. I fed the kitten with an eyedropper. It got so if he heard me, he would start mewing that kitten mew. I picked him up and told him he was sure a "yappy little guy." And that's where his name, Yappy, came from.

I found out later from the kids that his mother had been a pure Siamese and his father was a black Persian. They had gotten together by misadventure. It turns out that is some kind of special breed, too. As far as Yappy was concerned, I was his mother and father.

Are you getting the idea that Yappy was special? He was! And he thought he was a human and couldn't wait to grow up like me, that is, until I brought another cat home. Yappy took one look at her and ran. I heard him in the bathroom. He was on the counter looking at himself in the mirror. I guess it suddenly came to him that he was a cat and would remain like he was. He came out, drooped, and went and hid and wouldn't come out for a long time. I started praising him and telling him how wonderful and handsome he was. After a few weeks, he came around. Realizing he was a cat sure was a shock to him, though.

Carol and I had acquired a few more cats after we moved to Mesa, Arizona. Yappy was the leader and had rules of behavior for them. One night, I was feeling "snacky" and went to get a ham sandwich. As I got the meat out of the package with my usual grace, I dropped a piece. Since Carol was watching, the "5-second" rule did not apply, and I would have to throw it away. Yappy was watching what I did and yowled for a piece. I looked, and he was sitting up on his haunches. I tore off a small piece and gave it to him. He really liked it, although he usually disdained most "people food." He sat up again, so I tore off another piece and gave it to him. One of the other cats wandered in, saw what was going on, and yelled for his piece. Pretty soon, he had the idea that if he sat like Yappy, he would get a piece much quicker.

The next night, at 9:00 p.m. exactly, I went to get something from the fridge and there was Yappy. Carol had some pressed meat in there, so I thought to try that for a "treat." With the noise that Yappy and I made, the other cats soon assembled and were caterwauling for their share. I gave a treat to Yappy because he sat up and gave less to the others because they wouldn't. With me holding the meat over their heads, they were soon all sitting up.

At 9:00 every night, the cats would wander in from wherever they were. I soon taught them to catch the food when I threw it to them, or I would get it before they could and they'd have to do it again. Surprisingly, this was pretty easy.

If a cat wasn't present at 9:00 p.m., Yappy went to find him or her. He made them sit in a row and wait for their turn and be in the same order every time so everyone could catch it on their turn. Of course, they couldn't cheat and sit up early.

Yappy also learned to unlock doors. No, he didn't use a key. I'm talking about the kind of door that you can turn the knob to lock it. The apartment door was that way. The apartment was in a group of four. Three were in an "L" and one was on top of the center unit. Mine was the upstairs one. It had a small landing/porch and looked over the roofs of the other units.

I think Yappy started opening doors in an attempt to try to get the other cats to run off. To unlock the door, he would lean up and get the knob between his front paws. Using his claws he would turn the knob until the lock clicked, and then he would throw his weight back to pull the door slightly ajar. He would then drop down, grab it underneath, and hook it open. The other cats would run out on the porch and roofs and play. Yappy usually did this if I was gone too long (in his opinion). The first few times resulted in panic as I thought a burglar had broken in. Then I saw Yappy grinning at me and I knew.

If he was angry at me, Yappy would open all the drawers and doors in the apartment. He would then fish all the contents out onto the floor and leave it for me to clean up. Yappy hated a messy litter box. He had a special meow for that. Ignoring it was at your own peril. He would leave you a "reminder" to clean it in a place you couldn't ignore—your shoe or the bathroom sink. His ultimate revenge was leaving it on my pillow.

Yappy was not an ornery cat, he just insisted on being treated a certain way. He also guarded the house and his charges, the other cats. I ran a business out of my apartment and had a frequent delivery service. One driver, instead of knocking, just barged in. He got about two steps in before he was confronted by a miniature, black panther...19 pounds of hissing and growling Yappy. He quickly retreated. Another person who didn't believe what my black cat would do wound up needing stitches. I had a sign on the door that said, "Beware of Guard Cat." It was meant as a joke, but Yappy took it seriously. According to the cops, it exonerated me from liability.

Yappy watched over me. He would sleep on the bed with me, but would go do a patrol several times a night and come back. When I was sick, he would stand guard at the foot of the bed. If I had to throw up (I used to drink a bit), he would follow me and stay and watch me from a safe distance. His face showed concern and worry. He would go without food and not let the others bother me while I was sick. He would keep them off the bed. Only by my saying it was okay would he allow them up on the bed. If they weren't quiet, he would firmly force them off.

I had an ulcer that was not diagnosed until years later because it showed up as a high fever and a severe back pain that morphine couldn't touch. Yappy could tell I was coming down with it hours before I knew. He would herd the other cats away from me and from the bedroom. He would go and eat a snack from the dry food tower to prepare for a long watch. Usually, I was down for 24 to 48 hours. He stood watch all that time, and I never saw him nap once. He would just sit and worry.

Yappy would go for rides with me in my cars. He would sit with his hindquarters on the seat back and his front feet on my shoulder. Usually, it was on the inner side. If he saw something that offended him such as a dog in a truck, he would swap shoulders so he could growl at them. I would open the door of the apartment to go get Carol from work and Yappy would walk beside me to the car and assume his place. When we got home, he would lead us up the steps and wait for me to open the door. After Carol left us, we didn't go out too often anymore.

Late in his life, Yappy seemed to need to be held and rubbed a lot. I think he ached and liked the affection. A new batch of cats had come along. The others had died or gotten mellow, and we no longer did the 9:00 p.m. "treat." He just wanted to be near me all the time. I had remarried. She was a terrific woman named Mary. While he liked to torment her earlier in life, he now loved her, too. And I know she loved him in return.

I had to take a business trip to Detroit to speak at a convention, and I knew the end was near for Yappy. He was staggering and would have to stand and think about doing something before attempting it. He knew I was leaving, as he had all his life. He knew the suitcase meant I was going someplace. He hung around me and got all the pats I could give him. He purred like a young cat and dozed on my lap. I told him goodbye, a *real* goodbye, because I knew the end was near for him.

I arrived at my hotel in Detroit and was pulling the bag of things I used for my lecture through the deserted, long lobby. I had a sudden pain in my shoulder that brought me to my knees. It lasted for what seemed like hours, but was only 15 minutes by my watch. I wasn't especially worried about it, but noted the time. That evening when I called my wife, Mary, she said Yappy had died. I had known it before I called. It happened around the same time I had the pain. Our bond was so close that I just knew it. I cried like a baby for hours. I had to stay for two more miserable days in Detroit. It was April 1st, April Fools Day. Yappy had been born on the 4th of July, 23 years before. It had been a long, happy life. Those who knew him knew what an unusual cat he was. Arrogant and mischievous, loving and intelligent, he was a one of a kind and now my friend was gone. I still mourn him.

My son-in-law and daughter came over and helped my wife bury him. I don't know if I could have handled it. I was sorry I wasn't there for him, but I do think he waited for that opportunity. He didn't want to be remembered that way.

One week to the day after Yappy died, I had a massive heart attack and almost joined him. The paramedics and my poor wife kept me here. I had open-heart surgery to repair the damage. I guess I was pretty out-of-it for a while. I had pneumonia and spent many days in ICU. When I became more alert, I noticed something kept showing up in my peripheral vision. I would look and it was gone. One night, when I was off the pain meds, I woke up in the darkened room. I felt a presence that I knew. I heard a sound and looked in the direction it had come from. A pair of familiar eyes glowed back at me. I heard a purr that I knew. I couldn't mistake it.

A few nights later, when I was home and sleeping on the couch in the family room because I couldn't handle the waterbed, I felt a "trouncing" on my stomach. Trouncing is what I called the kneading a cat does with their paws when they are happy and purring. This usually happens just before they snuggle up and go to sleep. Yappy did that with me. It was almost his trademark. He was so mindless and pleased when he trounced that he drooled. After I felt the trouncing on my stomach, I felt moisture on my arm, but nothing was there when I tried to wipe it off.

Some nights, I can hear the meow Yappy used on his patrols. I have felt him nudge my hand for a rub as he used to in the old days. I try, but I can't touch him, even if I knew where to reach. No one else seems to hear him, except the few cats we have left. Yappy is the only one that is still here out of all we have had. I believe he is waiting for me to join him.

> I believe Yappy shows himself because I am closer to joining him.

After Yappy died, I started seeing shadows flit in my peripheral vision from time to time. They became familiar and welcome. But then, three years later, I had a stroke that disabled me. My vision was so messed up, I couldn't make out what was on the TV (when I could spot it, which wasn't often). I had been an artist, but that was gone. The fine control was missing and my detail was what had made me desirable to my clients. As I was reflecting on my losses one day, I felt a walking on the bed beside me. Suddenly, I could see my old black cat. I reached for him, but he stayed just out of reach. He had teased me that way while he was still alive. It proved to me it really was him. On that day, my eyes started to get better. They are not back to what they were, but at least I don't walk into walls quite as often.

I believe Yappy shows himself because I am closer to joining him. I no longer miss him. I miss petting him, having him trounce me, and feeling his sleekness under my hand. But I can't miss him because he is just over there. If you'll leave the room, I can hear him purr and see his yellow eyes glowing in the shadows. I have a lot of health problems, but I also have my best friend watching over me. I can't tell anyone I know or my family about him. I think they already believe the 'old man is a few bricks short of a load,' as it is. I don't know if they would believe me or not—and I don't really care. I know Yappy is with me still. I know when I go, I will have a friend to guide me to the Pearly Gates and if he can't come in with me, I won't go either.

"Writing is an all enveloping passion." From the time Steve Snider first saw a Hollywood-type writer, he has been in love

with the image of the tweed sport coat with patched sleeves, a straight stem pipe clenched in the teeth, and a Van Dyke goatee. He never saw one of those guys actually type a line, but they sure looked good in the movies. Steve wanted to be one, and as the saying goes, "Now I are! No goatee, full beard. No pipe, don't smoke. No tweed jacket, too hot and besides, I can type—well sorta."

19. Dad's Protection
Suzan L. Wiener

My luck started going from bad to worse in November, l986. That was the year my wonderful father (see photo 13 on page vi) passed away. How I adored him. He was so gentle and kind. Never a harsh word came from his lips. Tears fell when we had to say goodbye to him at his funeral. I wondered if I would ever see him again in the afterlife.

A few months later, my back went out. Diagnosed with a herniated disk, the doctor ordered complete bed rest for me. Afterwards, I was very limited in my daily activities, not being able to do anything that involved bending, lifting, or even sitting for long periods. To say I was depressed was an understatement. I couldn't work (I was a secretary and enjoyed my job) and doing anything physical was painful.

One night, I decided to try to take a hot shower. I turned on the water and warm steam began to fill the room. As I reached for the handrail my husband had installed by the shower to help steady myself, I felt a chill breeze across my body. Then, suddenly, it almost seemed like there was someone else in the room. I turned my head toward the steamed-up mirror. Through the mist, I saw what looked like the reflection of my father's face. I wasn't frightened, only stunned that he would appear this way.

Dad had always been a cautious man. He looked both ways when he crossed the street and was a stickler for obeying traffic rules when he drove. Many times, he had cautioned me to be careful doing this or to watch out for that, so I wasn't surprised by his ghostly presence. I just knew he had to be there to help me.

Before I had a chance to speak, I heard his easily recognizable deep voice calling out, "Sue, don't go into the tub!" There was no question it was him and his voice. Even though filled with caution, he was still as comforting and caring as when he had been alive.

Of course, I listened and didn't go into the shower. I was shaken by the incident and quickly left the bathroom. I went into the bedroom, sat down on my bed, and tried to calm myself. After a few minutes, I was calm enough to go back to the bathroom.

I discovered the entire bottom of the shower was covered in shampoo from a bottle that had fallen from the window shelf and cracked open. It had made it extremely slippery and, considering the shape I was already in, I would likely have fallen. I had a doctor's appointment that week and told him about what almost happened to me. I don't know if the doctor believed me, but he said that my father might have saved me from a lifetime in a wheelchair if I had fallen.

"Oh, thank you, Dad," I said gratefully to myself. I was sure he heard me. I now know that Dad will always be there for me in my time of need. And I know I will see my dad again.

Suzan L. Wiener has had numerous poems and several stories published in national magazines such as Mature Living, Saturday Evening Post, Complete Woman, Mocha Memoirs, *and more. She's been for writing for more than 10 years. Suzan also recently published her first love poetry e-book.*

20. When Spirits Use Signs
Peach Robidoux

Bah-hah! I'd laugh like a fool if you'd told me last year that I would be soon be writing about something like this. After death communication? Nonsense. I grew up Catholic for crying out loud; plus I'm as stubborn as heck. You could not make me believe that there is "another side," or that there's an open line to it. That is, until recently.

When I was a kid, I learned about Heaven, hell, purgatory, and limbo (for the un-baptized babies). I never accepted hell, purgatory, or limbo. And Heaven was, you know, pearly gates, seraphim, stuff like that. It was a cozy thought, although a bit hard to believe; too nebulous.

But I was taught what I was taught and was told not to question. The scientist in me giggled behind its hand at my faith. The poet in me wanted to know something beautiful was there. My whole being wanted someone to prove the afterlife one way or another because, in the back of my mind, no part of it really made sense. I was skeptical of all of them. Spirits? No. Hades? Bah! Not scientifically sound (and too scary).

As I grew, I searched. I studied other people's notions of the afterlife, but never fully believed in any of it. I wanted to, but it's hard to let go of what's familiar, even when it doesn't make sense. But faith is a funny thing. Belief is a funny thing. They were two sides of a funny coin. Sometimes, faith in a belief system is what gets a person through. Sometimes, it's breaking out of that system that gets her through. That's how it was for me.

I am afflicted with clinical depression. Most of the time, it sleeps in the back room of my brain. Occasionally, it awakens and trashes the house. Recently, it awoke and tried to burn the whole place down. It didn't. And though I can't be positive (what skeptic ever is?), I am fairly sure that communicating with my deceased grandparents (see photos 2 and 3 on page vi) helped me through the ordeal. Even now, my mind is laughing, "Yeah, right. Prove it." I can't. I can only tell what has happened to me and let others interpret as they choose.

A few months ago, my depression overwhelmed me with self-destructive thoughts. In desperation, I prayed for mercy to find a way out of my pain. I was certainly not going to ask my friends for help. My husband was already doing all he could and more. It was exhausting him. I knew I was loved, but felt so alone.

A healer friend came to me one day and said, "I've noticed that you've been out of sorts lately and I meditated about you. You'll tell me what's up if you need to, I'm sure. But the message I got is that you need to focus on the wisdom of your ancestors."

All right, I thought. What the heck does that mean? So I said, "What the heck does that mean?"

She told me, "When you pray or meditate, address your ancestors and ask them for guidance." Here's the trick: I had to suspend disbelief so that I might actually receive and understand the guidance. Me? Open up enough to pay attention? It seemed ridiculous. So I said, "This seems ridiculous."

My friend replied, "So, what harm could my way do? No one will see," I was so desperate, I would have belly danced on lava if it meant relief. So I tried it.

I meditate in my basement. I sit amidst the laundry and get some thinking done. There's never an audience except for a cricket or two, so why'd I feel so dumb thinking in a different way than usual? I did it anyway. I asked my grandparents to watch over me and to guide me out of this mess. I may even have been blushing. Was that cricket laughing? I gave myself the God-works-in-mysterious-ways pep talk. "You've got to get out there and be aware! Give it all you've got. Now, fight! Fight! FIGHT!"

Not long after that, things began to happen. Once, I went to change the load of laundry. As I was thinking about how hard life was being, a whiff of something vaguely familiar passed my nose. Pipe tobacco. No doubt about it. Immediately, I saw a picture in my head of my grandfather (Grampie) and felt calm for just a moment. Then it was gone. Okay, here's the thing. I remember almost nothing about Grampie because he died when I was four years old. So, I hadn't thought about him or his pipe tobacco in any real way ever. And no one in our house smokes. Was it a coincidence that I smelled that so soon after my prayer session? Was my mind playing tricks? Yes. Had to be. I dismissed it until I smelled it again a few days later in a different place, again nowhere near a place for smokers, and again when I was thinking suicidal thoughts.

> *As I grew, I searched. I studied other people's notions of the afterlife, but never fully believed in any of it. I wanted to, but it's hard to let go of what's familiar, even when it doesn't make sense.*

Okay, I thought. I'm open. I'm open. Nothing to be scared of. Just my mind!

When my Nana (Grampie's wife) was ill, she told some of us that if she could, she would come back as a cardinal. If she herself couldn't be one, she would see if she could send one our way to let us know she was thinking about us. I thought she was being facetious. Even though there have been family stories of a cardinal being around when serious or stressful events were happening, I didn't buy into the idea. It's a nice idea, but it does sound a little far-fetched, doesn't it? Nonetheless, it stuck in my brain and cardinals always remind me of Nana.

Once I got sick with depression and called upon my grandparents, I began to see cardinals everywhere. It could have just been that it was the right season for the little birds

> *I guess once I opened up and paid attention, the veil between the physical and spiritual worlds thinned.*

and they were on my mind, or maybe not. Either way, I thought of Nana and was comforted. After all, she suffered from depression, too, but was not in any position to let it show. She toughed it out. When I saw those birds, I thought of her strength.

As my illness progressed and suicidal thoughts plagued me almost constantly, a cardinal took up residence in my yard. Its call awoke me each morning at my backyard window. By the time I was up for work, the cardinal was near the kitchen, tweeting its crazy red head off. The bird swung vigorously and loudly on the bird feeder in the front yard near my car when I left for work. Its "tooweeet tweet tweet tweet tweet" would roll through my mind all day. With Nana's strength on my mind, I could struggle through another day. Was it coincidence that brought the bird right then? Who knows? I am beginning to think that coincidence is an over-rated concept.

If it had just been the smell and the dang bird, I might be able to dismiss it all. Then I had the dream. My Grampie sat smoking his pipe in his easy chair. He nodded his head, soothing, and said, "By and by, by and by." Earlier that day, I had been meditating about the question: when will I find the right doctor and treatment plan? That dream gave me a little boost of faith and courage (even if it did scare me a little).

Eventually, I did find that golden treatment combination after a rather close call with death. As my husband stopped me from hurting myself, I heard him shouting and I heard me crying. I heard the call of the cardinal and the words, "by and by," swirling loudly, softly, loudly in my mind. I could not go through with it. I flopped over, exhausted and alive. Since then, I have been recovering and following the treatment plan. Were my encounters with my grandparents coincidences or real? To me, they were real.

My cardinal still lives in my yard and seems to get loud when I have a particularly difficult day. I've let myself become open to possibility. This has all made me humble. I'm reminded that I do not have the answers. I can't know for sure what's on the other side, whether there is a Heaven or simply a different plane or what. I can't know for sure whether these communications were real or just some construct of my mind. Frankly, I'm not up for questioning it just now. Let's just say I am not so skeptical any more—at least about that. There are so many new thoughts and ideas sparked from these past few months. It hasn't been easy; but being in contact with my grandparents has reminded me that I am blessed and I've inherited the tools to fight anything in the future. I guess once I opened up and paid attention, the veil between the physical and spiritual worlds thinned. I know I'm never alone. I don't have to face life by myself. That's too important an idea to ignore or be wary of. So what if I was wrong before? So what if there is such a thing as after-death communication? (And I'm pretty sure there is.) I can't let it go. Even I'm not that stubborn.

Peach Robidoux is a veteran middle school reading and writing teacher and has a fabulous, kooky husband and 4-year-old daughter combo. "I play a lousy banjo and I look exactly as my name Peach suggests—short, red-haired, and roundish."

21. They Come to Take Us Home
Anna Teague

My dad always talked with admiration about his brother, my Uncle Mike. Like my dad, he served in the Vietnam war. He was a medic and, in an attempt to save some lives, was blown up by a hand grenade and recognizable only by his dog tags. But unlike my dad, he never returned home.

Uncle Mike's death tore my Grandmom apart. She grew distant and distraught to the point of suicide attempts. Since my granddad was a bus driver, he was on the road a lot, spending a couple of days away from home at a time. I guess he took comfort in knowing that my family only lived a house away.

My brother was playing in his room one day when he clearly heard someone say, "Something's wrong with Mom." He looked around and saw no one, so he went to find our mom. He thought she might have walked over to visit Grandmom so he scurried off to see. The backdoor was open so he went in and there, passed out and lying on the floor in a pool of blood, was Grandmom. He ran for help. It turns out she had taken some pills and had slit a wrist. Had it not been for those four words, "Something's wrong with Mom," Grandmom would have died.

I heard about what had happened, but never really thought much about it. I guess it was because Mike was born before my time and I never got the chance to know him.

I've always been fascinated with Ouija® boards (also known as Talking Boards) and séances and had an undying desire to scare my cousins to pieces when they came down to visit. Since our house wasn't that big, they stayed at my grandparents' house.

It was dark outside and everyone was playing cards in the kitchen. My two cousins and I went into the hall and closed all the doors. We decided to try to do a séance and have a chat with Uncle Mike. To our surprise, one of the doors opened when we called his name. We sprouted wings underneath our shoes and ran straight into the kitchen, where everyone was still playing cards. He scared us to death; so much so, the hair on my arms was standing on end. He seemed to be reaching out and we were being chickens.

> *He suddenly bolted upright and there, at the foot of his bed, was my Uncle Mike, standing there staring at him.*

Granddad wasn't one to hallucinate or make up things. He was a practical and stable man, not the kind of person to get stirred up easily.

One night, he had gone to bed sleeping quite soundly. He suddenly bolted upright and there, at the foot of his bed, was my Uncle Mike, standing there staring at him. He looked over to see if Grandmom was awake. She wasn't. It really shook him up and, for the rest of the night, he couldn't go back to sleep. He shared what had happened the next day with Grandmom. Later, he shared his experience with my dad.

Granddad passed away from a heart attack a few years later. Once more, pain had struck my Grandmom. The rocking chair where Granddad used to sit and watch television with her looked vacant and empty. Every evening, they had enjoyed a favorite game show together while sometimes popping popcorn to snack on. All she could do now was stare at that lonely spot where happier times were memories.

One evening, it was time to watch the game show. Grandmom settled in to watch it. She looked at the rocking chair and there was Granddad, sitting in it like he had always done when he was alive. She knew then that he was okay and that he would always love her. Life wasn't empty anymore. She felt renewed.

> Grandmom started talking to Granddad and Uncle Mike. She turned to the sitter and asked if she saw them.

Grandmom eventually became ill with congestive heart failure and had to have a round-the-clock sitter in her home. In the early hours one morning, she seemed to be okay. But her passing was not far away. Grandmom started talking to Granddad and Uncle Mike. She turned to the sitter and asked if she saw them. The sitter didn't. This conversation was for Grandmom's ears only. They had come to take her to her new home.

Anna Teague was born in a "teeny town" in Texas and has worked with the mentally challenged and disabled. She is passionate about birds and has enjoyed modeling, ballet, and belly dancing. Anna plays the piano and the flute, sings and acts, and has always loved writing. To encourage, inspire, and create hope in people is the motivation that keeps her writing.

EDITOR'S NOTE: You can read more about Talking Boards at http://www.museumoftalkingboards.com.

22. Prayers Are Heard
Marina Alcasas

One night, a slight breeze and bright light woke me up from a sound sleep. As I opened my eyes, I was shocked to see my grandmother (see photo 36 on page viii), who passed away the previous year, sitting on the edge of my bed.

"Grandma!" I whispered, caring not to wake my sleeping husband, "How? Are you really here?"

Grandma smiled and placed her hand on my husband's shoulder. "Don't worry, child. He will sleep peacefully till morning. But you have to get up now. Your parents will be in an accident in a few minutes; they will need your prayers and help."

I got off the bed and fell onto my knees in desperation. "Please, God," I pleaded, "If this accident is really unavoidable, please do not make it fatal! Please help my parents not to be hurt too bad and send them any sort of help they will need right away!"

Praying was the last thing I remembered the next morning. As soon as I opened my eyes, I ran to the phone with my hands shaking uncontrollably, hoping that what I saw was just another paranoid daughter's dream.

My father picked up the phone. "Hi, honey," he said, unusually cheerful, "How are things going for you there?"

Relieved to hear his voice, but still not sure what to think of the previous night's vision, I asked to talk to my mother. "She-ee— she can't come to the phone right now," my father quickly answered.

"Why not?" I questioned.

"She's—in the shower." my father answered, and his tone of voice made it obvious to me that he was trying to hide something.

"Okay, Dad, what is it?" I demanded, "What's happening?"

> *It is comparatively easy for a spiritually sensitive individual to hear from any spirit, not just a godly one.*

He took a deep breath and said quietly, "Her ribs are broken, honey."

I slipped onto the chair, feeling the room starting to spin around me.

My father continued, "She can't come to the phone because she is in bed. She just fell asleep after being in pain for hours and I do not dare to wake her. Last night, as we were driving back from your aunt's, a drunk driver slammed into our car practically head-on. By a miracle, I managed to steer the car a bit to the side, but we were still hit pretty bad and our car is so bad there is nothing to fix. I got out of the ordeal with hundreds of cuts and bruises, but nothing serious. Your mother, on the other hand, had broken almost all her ribs and had to be taken to the hospital immediately after the accident. Thankfully, an ambulance drove by seconds after we crashed, and she hadn't lost much blood. The doctors told me that if she was not helped within the first half hour she might not have made it. It was a miracle we both survived."

After I came to my senses from the initial shock, I asked my father when the accident had happened. It was at exactly the time when my grandma showed up instructing me to pray for them. A chilly thought crept into my mind: What if I had not listened? What if I had brushed it aside as a silly dream and chosen not to pray?

My father was right: it was a miracle that saved them, a miracle of God's power brought down by my grandmother's caring hands.

Many churches today condemn the practice of speaking with spirits and even receiving prophecies from God as a spiritually dangerous and even ungodly practice. On one hand, this is not completely unreasonable. It is comparatively easy for a spiritually sensitive individual to hear from any spirit, not just a godly one. However, just like it would be ridiculous to quit reading anything just because there are some bad books on the market, it does not seem wise to stop receiving all spiritual messages for fear of ever tuning in to the wrong spirit guide.

I believe that not all departed spirits are forced to go straight to Heaven or hell. The Bible talks about "Hades," which was translated as "hell," but in the original Hebrew, means "ghostly, unseen state." Some spirits may have unfinished business and remain on earth for some time. Some are bound to the place where they lived, and some occasionally return in spirit to help their families and other loved ones through dreams, visions, or occasional ghostly appearances, just like my dear grandmother did.

There is a multitude of Bible stories about people receiving guidance in dreams, visions, or audible instructions from angels and spirits guides and, just like God used those helpful spirits in the days past, today we can also partake of the wealth of wisdom stored up in Heaven—if we have faith to listen and courage to try.

Marina Alcasas is a freelance Christian writer whose work has been published in a number of online and print family magazines such as Christian Families Online, Eve, *and* Bible Advocate Online. *She also writes and edits content for the children's online magazine* Alvin's Tent *and gives free email Bible classes about prophecy and the spirit world. You can read more about* Alvin's Tent *at http://www.activatedla.com.*

23. "I Saw Daddy!"
Jozette Aaron

Y ES—I kept telling myself over and over. He's dead, you're tired, and soon it will all seem like a bad dream.

I was 26 at the time—a brand new widow with two small children—wondering how to tell them their daddy was dead. It didn't go well at all. My daughter, who was seven at the time, could not accept this and blamed me. My son, a 3-year-old, had no reaction at all.

As I struggled to put our lives back together, I was assailed with visions of my dead spouse. Along with those visions came the memories of subtle threats and implied danger. Ours was a turbulent relationship, fraught with physical, emotional, and mental abuse of the worse kind.

The words, "I'll take you to hell with me!" pounded in my ears. I was as frightened by those words then as I was at the memory of just how unsafe and unprotected I'd felt.

For years, I lived in fear for my life and the lives of my children. They were too young to realize what was happening when they heard shouting and screaming. When they'd enter a room that served as the battlefield of the moment, I'd tell them that "Mommy and Daddy are only playing," and then quickly remove them and me from the house. The tears often stuck in my throat because there was no releasing them. One didn't cry if one was only playing, did they?

He died as violently as he lived, at the age of 31, casting me instantly into the role of widow and breadwinner. Having been a stay-at-home mother, I lacked the skills needed to secure a job that paid enough to support the three of us in New York City in the 1970s.

I took any job that offered training and managed to keep us floating. It was hard to do this and deal with clinical depression, which had me living in a vacuum and suffering panic attacks. A visit to the doctor and my return home with a prescription for Valium® made me mad as hell. I asked for help, not pills!

Realizing that my life had reduced me to a 26-year-old pill-popping widow made me flush all of them down the toilet and make the decision to get on with bettering my life and the lives of my children. I felt free of the abuse, but was I really free?

The first of several visits occurred just two weeks after he'd passed and, of course, all I could think was that I was finally cracking up!

I was sitting up and reading in bed one night. A bedside lamp provided the only light in the room. It suddenly became too dark to read and I thought the bulb was beginning to burn out. As I started to get out of bed to go in search of a replacement, a chill caught the back of my neck like an ice cold fingertip drawing a line slowly across warm flesh. With an audible whimper and an indrawn breath, I saw him, emerging from the corner behind a partially closed door. A bright orange seemed to light his path as he emerged in black trousers and his favorite sweater. I thought that odd as I swallowed my fear, "He wasn't buried in those."

Sure, you say. This lady is nuts! I assure you I'm not!

I drew back and watched as he walked towards the foot of the bed and, when he reached out, I saw the palms of his hands flatten as though they had made contact with glass. The look on his face was one of astonishment, as though surprised he could not touch me; my own mirroring the fear that gripped me as I again heard those words he'd said while still living, "I'll take you to hell with me!"

He made his way around to the side of the bed nearest me, his hands working up and down this invisible wall, palms flat and blanching from the resistance he encountered as he went, frantically trying to find a way to reach me.

"Oh God—he's going to take me with him!" my mind screamed as I watched in terror. My head was pounding and my throat closed around the silent screams rising up inside of me.

Frozen in fear, all I could do was watch as he inched closer and closer. Not knowing what barred his way, I also didn't know if it would continue to protect me from this touch.

Finally, after finding no way to make contact, he retraced his steps and, with one last look at me, backed into the corner from which he emerged. As the orange glow faded, he disappeared.

I opened my mouth to scream, but nothing came out. I got out of bed and ran to my children's room. They were sleeping soundly. I went down the hall toward the living room, flicking on lights along the way. Afraid to return to my room, I sat out the rest of the night in the middle of the living room floor, intent on watching over me and mine, afraid to sleep and, at the same time, afraid of what would happen if he returned.

The first time my head made contact with the floor was just enough of a nudge to make me return to my bed. Leaving on the main lights, I finally fell into a deep sleep, unable to stay awake any longer. When I woke up, I would have thought I'd dreamt it all except for the glare of the lights and two slightly bruised thighs; bruising as a result of me pinching myself as I watched him stalk me. I shuddered over and over, as though my body had been robbed of warmth.

Two nights passed and I waited and watched. Fear was a constant bedmate now and sleeping was the result of exhaustion after staring into the night, watching for signs of his return.

On the third day, in the morning, as I rolled over in bed, I opened my eyes and found him lying next to me, staring through glassy, lifeless eyes. I made a short, fearful sound, scrambling to the far side of the bed, and reached for the light on the bedside table. When I clicked it on, I discovered that he was gone, an indent evident in the pillow where his head had been.

Chilled to my very core and angry at how he continued to invade my life and my sense of security even from the grave, I yelled into the silence, "Am I to have no peace?" Reaching across, I grabbed up the proof of his visit and tossed it across the room.

> A few of the other students and my teacher all approached me after the class to tell me of their own experiences and fears saying that they, too, had not told another soul.

I saw him only a couple of times over the next four weeks. Each time, I felt less threatened, yet remained fearful. He seemed to just want to look at me; he made no further efforts to touch me.

His visits stopped as suddenly as they had started. He was finally gone! I didn't tell anyone about this experience at that time because I already suspected that I had lost a marble or two. I didn't want to draw attention to this most troubling turn of events. I went through the next seven years trying to come to terms with this phenomenon and it wasn't until I made a speech in college about strange and unexplained occurrences that some light was shed on me. I wasn't alone. A few of the other students and my teacher all approached me after the class to tell me of their own experiences and fears saying that they, too, had not told another soul.

This experience caused me to think long and hard about my life and, when I thought about my past, my grandmother came to mind. I spent a lot of time with her as a child, but we usually didn't communicate with words. We had a way of communicating with one another that was more telepathic than verbal. When I grew up and got married, I took my first born to see her. She took my hand in hers and gently turned my palm up. After studying it for several minutes, she looked at me, told me I'd be a widow, I'd also be divorced, and that I'd have four children and be wealthy in my older years.

Not ever having experienced this before, I didn't pay much attention to it. My husband asked that his palm be read. Grandma looked at his palm for just a few seconds before telling him she couldn't read his palm because of the calluses on it.

He was dead seven years later.

I started having dreams about things that would actually occur later. This was pretty scary since one involved the death of a friend. I dreamt she had died in her apartment. And she died the next day, in her apartment—the scene playing out exactly like the dream.

The next night, I dreamt that my son was in a playground with a group of children and that there was an accident. In my dream, I was told that someone was hurt, although they didn't know whom at the time. I went outside and, as I ran toward the playground, I noticed a crowd of neighbors running in the same direction. As I drew closer to the park, the crowd became larger, and I had to push my way through in order to see what they were looking at. Just as I reached the area where my son was playing, I woke up, a shudder running through me because I didn't know the ending.

Later that morning, I had to go to the grocery store and my son had asked permission to wait for me in the playground. As it was on my way, I gave permission, telling him not to wander, "I won't be long."

A short time later, as I made my way in the direction of the playground, I noticed a group of the neighbors running in the same direction I was going in. Keeping pace with them and wondering why their clothing looked familiar, I asked what was happening.

"Couple o' kids got hurt in the playground."

Heart pounding and with the sudden awareness that this was my dream, I ran faster than I ever thought I could. Pulling and tugging at the sleeves of people while asking them to let me through, I finally emerged from the crowd.

There sat my son—holding the hand of his friend who had his knee blown off when someone threw a large firecracker into the concrete barrel they were playing in, not knowing the kids were inside.

> *"Mom, Mom, I saw him! I saw Daddy, Mom!"*

I was afraid to sleep after those experiences. I became more of a recluse, not wanting anyone to see me falling apart because I was sure I was having a breakdown.

Nothing else happened for many more years. I remarried and had the last two of my four children before that marriage ended in divorce. My older two children now had children of their own and no other dreams or visitations had occurred. Life, at last, was settling down.

Then, on a lazy summer afternoon, my phone rang and, as I lifted the receiver, I could hear the frantic shouting of my daughter.

"Mom, Mom, I saw him! I saw Daddy, Mom!"

"I know sweetheart. I've seen him, too!"

"You have? When?" And as I told her the story, she became less afraid and more curious. I reassured her that he just wanted to see her and to make sure she was okay.

"He was wearing all white—does that mean he's an angel now?"

"Maybe," was all I could say.

She saw him only once more after that and then he was gone.

He's been gone for 28 years now and, in that time, I have done a lot of reading and research on the study of spirits and their existence in our lives. My grandmother was very influential in guiding my path in my younger years, enabling me to be receptive to the awakening I am now experiencing. One thing for certain is that death is not the end of life. It is both the end of one life and the beginning of another.

Jozette Aaron is a published author (also writing as Georgie DeSilva) and freelance writer. She is the editor-in-chief and publisher of **DeSilva's News**, a monthly e-zine, which is a tool writers rely on to meet their creative needs. She has been published in four anthologies, the most recent by Adams Media, and is marketing one of four novels she has completed. She has her own website, The Authors Desk, at http://www.theauthorsdesk.com and can be contacted by email at editor@theauthorsdesk.com. Jozette resides in Ontario, Canada.

24. Dad Returns With Advice
Ray Austin Kampa

I dialed Ruby Ann's number and waited for her to pick up. It had been years since we had talked on the phone and, since our mother's recent death from rapidly acting cancer, we had promised each other that we'd stay in touch. She picked up the phone and, when I said, "Hi, Rubes," there was a long pause.

"Ray, is that you?" she asked in a soft, cautious way that was uncharacteristic of her usual brightness.

Chuckling, I answered, "Sure, it's me. Who did you think?"

She let out her breath. "Oh," she laughed, "You sounded just like Dad! I didn't know what to think."

This telephone conversation happened back in the early 1990s. Our father (see photo 19 on page vi) had passed from this world in a freak automobile accident in 1977. You can imagine why Rubes might have felt hesitance when she heard from her youngest brother, whose voice had mellowed over the years to resemble our father's. As we kept on talking, more things came out. She had experienced many dreams where Dad came to visit, offering advice for the problems she had been dealing with.

This time, I was silent for a longer period than usual. Should I tell her? I decided maybe not right away, as our conversation turned to more mundane things. We talked about her kids and grandkids, plans for retirement to the coast of Oregon, how I was doing in my job, and what the East Coast was like. I was living in Virginia at the time, near Washington D.C., while she was living near Sacramento, California.

Then, as our conversation wore down, I decided to bring up the subject.

"Rubes, did you know I have had many dreams similar to yours? What do you suppose is going on? Is that really Dad coming to visit, or is it just our imaginations?"

My sister pondered this for a moment. "Ray," she said without a hint of condescension, "I think it is a sign from our Lord that Dad is in Heaven and is okay." My sister is very religious, Roman Catholic. I asked if she remembered shining eyes and a yellow or white glow, and we agreed on those details—also that Dad often appeared in the setting of a workshop or walking through a wooded area. But, what about the advice? How good was it?

Some of it, for my sister, was to simply have faith and move on. Yet, I remembered details regarding specific problems I was dealing with at the time and even a few premonitions about future events. Was it that I was psychic, was my father actually talking to me, or was it, indeed, some powerful spirit providing assurance? I am not particularly religious, just spiritual. My possibilities did not need to be set into a dogmatic structure like Heaven and earth, God and angels.

Rubes has no doubt. Her faith is strong. I, on the other hand, could imagine that my father might be earning his wings, so to speak. I remember him as a fiercely independent man who loved to learn and tinker. He was also well-loved in the small, northern Minnesota town in which we lived, due to his willingness to help people and take barter—a sweater, garden vegetables, frozen walleye or northern pike—in return for his ability to fix televisions, refrigerators, and just about anything else around the house.

Had my father gone toward the light, touched the face of God, and taken on further responsibilities from the other side? Had he become a guiding angel for his family and perhaps others? This makes perfect sense to me. My dreams were rich with my father's presence during the mourning period after his death and for years more, as I struggled to make my way in the world. Then there's the fact that both my sister and I had experienced the same thing, often with the same imagery. Could this have simply been a genetic preponderance for having vividly real dreams, some of which turn prophetic?

Perhaps our shared experiences with my father while he lived led to common images in our dreams.

Well, skeptics have plenty of ammunition for this. After all, we only know the world through our senses and imaginations, or "consciousnesses," if you will.

> After all, we only know the world through our senses and imaginations, or "consciousnesses," if you will.

Some religions claim that life itself is an illusion and that only the spirit is real. Renee Descartes said, "I think, therefore I am," and "I can doubt everything, except one thing, and that is the very fact that I doubt."

Sometimes, though, we have to put a stake in the ground and accept that something has actually happened. For my sister, she doesn't believe that she had any direct communication from our father. That is her right as a free-thinking American to determine just what she wants to believe, and I feel strongly that her interpretation is every bit as good as mine. One of the powerful things in our sibling relationship is this ability to disagree on detail, yet agree on the core subject. I wish more of us could do that.

I choose to believe that my father was communicating with me directly through dreams. My dreams can be so realistic that I'll wake up wondering if those events really happened. Strictly speaking, the dream itself certainly happened within my brain, but is there a spiritual world just outside our conceptions of the material world? Could this spiritual world be tapped into through dreams, or could spirits delivery prophetic messages through dreams?

When my father came to visit and guide, there was no other purpose. It was just to contact a son who was lost in the wilderness and to point to a possible new direction. He had left this earth so suddenly, an instant death, his chest crushed into the steering wheel of a vehicle that, for no apparent reason, left the road and hit a tree. So many issues had not been put to rest. I know my father and he isn't one to just sit around playing

> The ideas on what happens with spirit stuff are as varied as the tongues spoken on earth.

harps and singing hymns all through eternity, let me tell you that. When he did play music, he yodeled to shake the house! He loved Hank Williams, and I can see him now, his thickly muscled arms around an old Gibson guitar, playing hard to be heard with the fiddles, a 1930s style hat cocked with attitude, his tall lineman's boots stomping time at the old barn dances.

Then my mind's eye sees him hunched over a neighbor's television set at our kitchen table, the acrid smoke from burning solder flux curling around his head. My mother sits in the dining room watching the old black-and-white set. Perry Mason is on. She knew how to take it easy after a hard day's work, but not my father. No, my father would have wanted to go to work immediately after his death, to straighten things out, and to make sure his family was doing well before he moved on to other projects. My father liked projects and often had several going all at once, much to my mother's irritation. I hear her now, calling from the dining room, asking when he'd be finished with that darn TV. The soldering is stinking up the house, she'd complain. Then Dad would put away his tools and comply. She didn't really care about the solder smell. She just wanted his company.

Interestingly enough, both Rubes and I stopped having dreams about our father at about the same time. It was as if his job had been completed, and now he could do whatever spirits on the other side do. Some say you join the Lord in Heaven, some say you eventually join with an over soul or great spirit, and some say this happens through multiple incarnations as humans or even animals and plants. The ideas on what happens with spirit stuff are as varied as the tongues spoken on earth.

We have no way of testing any of this scientifically and, for those who think only with the scientific method, it is quite impossible for me to have communicated directly with my father's spirit. After all, how does one prove the existence of spirit? It has no mass, no dimension; there's nothing measurable about it.

Yet, I know my father talked with me. Maybe it was a bigger spirit passing notes to me from my father, like surreptitious students in a classroom. Fine, that works, too. The point of the matter is that I received more mature advice from my dreams than I could have dreamt up myself. I think this might be a touchstone of communication with another consciousness. Is the communication outside of you? Are these thoughts distinctly unique enough that you are sure they have come from a separate consciousness? Well, at least one with distinct personality, I suppose, since some would argue that we are all part of the same consciousness. I'll accept that as well because, in the end, the results are the same.

Here's an example of the advice my father rendered: When I was working in a warehouse in 1977, after his death, I had a dream where my father asked if I was happy with my job. I told him that I was not and wanted to do something better in the world. He told me to go shopping at one of the local malls and check out the bookstore. That weekend I went to the mall. The season was near Christmas.

I thought I might buy books for some people this time around, rather than the usual trash. In the bookstore, I found the answer to my job dissatisfaction: a job-hunting manual different from any other. It was titled *What Color Is Your Parachute? A Practical Manual for Job-Hunters and Career-Changers* and written by Richard Bolles, a very spiritual and practical person. I bought the book and, by springtime, I had a new job in computers.

Coincidence? Perhaps. But the fact that I had many dreams about conversations with my father during this major

> In the case of my father, disbelief in his existence on the other side would not stop that existence. Only the communication with him would cease to exist.

transition says something and, to my sister and I, the message is very simple: Our father loves us very much and did what he could to help us from the other side. When we ended our telephone conversation about this, we both felt closer and very lucky to have had a father like ours. Even now, we sense a presence every now and then, and we know that Dad has just dropped by to visit. Or, as my sister likes to put it, the Lord has come by to give reassurance.

How certain can I be about this? If we consider what Descartes said about doubt, the only certainty is the fact that we doubt. From there, we need to judge what to believe from all the sensory inputs we get. If I stub my toe, my pain gives a strong impression of the reality, yet that pain would not exist if the nerve pathways from my toe to my brain were to be severed. So what would happen if I severed a pathway from spirituality to my beliefs? Would the spirituality stop existing? Actually, no, just as my toe wouldn't stop existing if the nerve pathways were to be severed—just the pain would stop existing. In the case of my father, disbelief in his existence on the other side would not stop that existence. Only the communication with him would cease to exist.

But does my father's spirit actually exist, or is this just something my imagination created while in the throes of mourning? I frankly can't prove that my father's spirit exists, just as nobody can prove that God or any other spirit exists. I can prove that my toe exists though, at least by consensus. I see my toe; you see my toe. My sister saw my father; I saw my father. I think this has at least as much credence—and perhaps if a survey were to be taken, others may have seen our father in their dreams, too.

Still, my point is not to convince you that my father's spirit exists. I'm just trying to explain how this is a possibility and how strange and beautiful it was that my sister and I had very similar dream experiences. Now we communicate mostly through email. Our relationship as siblings has grown very strong over the years, and both of us contribute much of this growth to our common experiences with Dad after he passed.

*Ray Austin Kampa grew up in Northern Minnesota, leading a childhood life that rivals any of Mark Twain's characters. He enjoyed hunting grouse and fishing the many area lakes, camping out, and especially exploring by motorcycle once he came of age. Ray is a twice-published author (*Unix Storage Management, *ISBN 1-59059-029-5; and* Deer in the Headlamps: Out of Work at Fifty Years of Age, *ISBN 1-4137-0667-3), a freelance writer, and a Unix systems administrator.*

25. Midnight's Last Visit
Howard Wiener

Before marrying my present wife, Suzan, I was married to Terri for two years. At first, our marriage was a happy one, but then things started going wrong.

I loved our cat, Midnight (see photo 24 on page vi), and spoiled him rotten. Any extra money I had went to buy him toys and gourmet cat food. His contented purr and healthy coat affirmed that spoiling him was not in vain. I played with Midnight frequently, and he loved the foil ball I threw for him. He was such a wonderful pet and helped me get through my days.

As Terri and I began to drift apart, Midnight seemed to sense my unhappiness. He stayed around me more and comforted me. After months of arguing, Terri and I decided to get a divorce. We tried a separation, but we knew a divorce was inevitable. It was a very sad time for me. I wanted to take Midnight with me, but could only afford a small studio apartment where pets were not allowed.

I tried to find another apartment, to no avail. On the day I moved, I couldn't even say goodbye to Midnight. It was too emotional for me. Tears welled up in my eyes, but I brushed them away. A grown man wasn't supposed to cry.

One night, about six months later, I fell into a troubled sleep. I missed Midnight terribly and felt guilty for leaving him. After tossing and turning restlessly, I suddenly opened my eyes to see Midnight's bright green eyes staring into mine!

I was startled and wondered how he had found his way to my studio apartment. Midnight's soft purring made me happier than I had been in a long time. I reached out to stroke him but, in an instant, he was gone. That night was the first good sleep I'd had in months.

The next morning, the phone rang. It was Terri. Her sobbing voice warned me something was seriously wrong. The hair on the back of my neck stood up in trepidation. She told me Midnight had suffered a heart attack and died instantly. A chill ran through me. Gathering up my courage, I asked her what time he had died. Somehow I knew she was going to say 12:30 that morning—the exact time Midnight had come to say goodbye to me. It was his way of letting me know he wasn't angry that I couldn't take him with me.

I will never forget that moment. It made me realize that someday I will be with Midnight again.

Howard Wiener has been published in national magazines such as The Saturday Evening Post *and* The National Enquirer.

26. Heeding Dad's Warning
Jeanne Yorga

One morning, my dad he called me on the phone and said "Just wanted to tell you I will always love you." He died later that day, in the afternoon, alone.

After his death, Dad came to me often in dreams, giving me messages for others. But this night—this night was different, and it wasn't a dream.

It was approximately 9:30 p.m. on an early September evening. I was sitting on the couch in my living room watching *Touched By An Angel* and eating a large salad with Italian dressing. I was starting to get full, and noticed I had no cigarettes for my after dinner smoke.

The store was two blocks away, it was dark outside, and my garage light was burned out. But I wanted that smoke.

I got up from the couch to put away the leftover salad and proceeded through the dining area. When I came around the corner, I was so shocked by what I saw that I screamed. My arms went in the air and so did the salad bowl. It hit the ceiling leaving lettuce, Italian dressing, and whatever else in the bowl on the ceiling, walls, countertops, and the floor.

There, blocking the front door, stood Dad, dressed in his gray slacks and cream-colored, button down, short-sleeved shirt looking like he did in the pictures from the 1950s, not the 90s, when he died.

I yelled "Don't you ever scare me like that again! Cough or something so I'll know you're there. You could give a person a heart attack like that. Dad. Why are you here?"

He stepped back and crossed his arms in that stern way he had. He then shifted his eyes towards the bedroom. I heard him in my mind or head say, "Go into the bedroom."

I replied, "I was just going to the store for more cigs."

He said more sternly, "Go."

I went in the bedroom and found a half smoked cig in the ashtray. "Funny, Dad, but this isn't going to make it."

At that moment, from my open bedroom window, I heard someone yell, "Stop! Police! Or I'll Shoot!"

> There, blocking the front door, stood Dad, dressed in his gray slacks and cream-colored, button down, short-sleeved shirt looking like he did in the pictures from the 1950s, not the 90s, when he died.

I forgot all about dad. My stomach was doing flip-flops. I quickly turned off the bedroom light and tried to listen. I then went back into the hall, and Dad was still standing by the door; I then knew why he'd come to visit. He smiled, pointed, blew me a kiss, and said, "Remember, I'll always love you." And with a wave, he disappeared.

I found out later that there was a man in the neighborhood who was stalking his ex-girlfriend at work two blocks away. He'd planned to kill her. The police were after him, and the chase ended by my garage. If Dad hadn't stopped me from walking out the front door, I'd have walked right in between the police and the assailant.

Dad once promised me he would always be there when I needed him. I know now it's not for the things I can handle, but for the situations I can't manage or things I don't know about.

Jeanne Yorga, a writer and poet, was raised in Minnesota along with eight other siblings. She has experienced several spiritual occurrences and enjoys learning about the unseen world around her.

27. Moster Henny's Ring
Michelle Porter

I'm frequently told that I am a sensitive person. Until recently, my usual reaction to such a comment had been to rise to the defensive with, "I am NOT!" In this corporate-oriented culture, sensitivity is often equated with being a crybaby, a softie, or one who is easily riled. Though my feelings are pretty easily hurt, and I admit that I don't take criticism well, being "sensitive" widens my field of vision to this world. Unlike those who view things in basic black and white, I don't need a book to teach me how to stop and smell the roses; I'm already focused on the bumblebee perusing soft-pink petals.

Several months ago, just before the winter holidays, I experienced something so remarkable that I no longer cringe at the sensitive remark; I revel in its blessings.

My mother was born in Denmark and was the youngest of three much older siblings. They had already married and established families of their own when mom immigrated to the United States in 1952. Mom met Dad and they were married. Soon, they'd built a home in Newton, Massachusetts, which they added rooms to as the children came. I arrived first, adopted as an infant. Then came my sister, also adopted and, finally, a boy of their own. Mom was very happy in her role as stay-at-home mom and homemaker and she did a great job! But being so far from her family in Denmark was emotionally difficult. "Ma Bell" hadn't yet made it easy or inexpensive to "reach out and touch someone" and the majority still traversed the Atlantic by ocean liner, taking several days to cross. But cross we did, by ship and plane, several times in my youth.

When I was two years old, Mom and I sailed for Denmark. Like any new mother, she was proud and eager to show me off to her family. That was the first time I met Moster Henny (see photos 4 and 11 on page vi and photo 26 on page viii). Moster is "mother's sister" in Danish. One look was all it took; we were bonded. Moster Henny had a smile that could warm the Russian army. Her face was so full of the joy of life that the language barrier we had meant absolutely nothing. We communicated very well. One time, when I stubbornly refused to go to bed in the crib set up for me, she just climbed in and sat there laughing and eating a piece of cucumber, which got everybody laughing. There were other visits, on both sides of the ocean, but we started a correspondence when I was barely able to hold a pencil. Initially, with my mother's help, I would carefully write the words on paper. Moster Henny always started her notes and letters with: "My Little Darling."

And so it came to pass that, again, a call came from Denmark, while my mother was in her home so far away, that my dearest Moster Henny had died. There was no time to rush home, no time to say goodbye. She had never let on how sick with cancer she had been.

Her one and only son, Mads, sent my mother some jewelry Henny had, and my mother and I sat down one evening to take a look at it. One was a gold signet ring that Moster Henny never took off her little finger. Mom gave it to me and told me that the enclosed letter instructed her to do so. I put it on. Perfect fit.

Boy, I was so happy to have that ring! The gold was warm on my hand and every time I looked at it, I could think of my beloved aunt. Then one day I took it off (I don't remember why), and couldn't find it again where I thought I'd left it. A thorough search of my premises revealed nothing. I was devastated over the loss, but had to admit my own stupidity in leaving it about in a household with three cats who might have found it an amusing trinket.

One evening before Christmas, I was sitting on my sofa writing some cards and listening to the radio when I felt another presence in the room with me. It was as if someone had sat down beside me and I could feel the warmth from that. Then, I started thinking about Moster Henny. Thinking led into actually seeing her face as if a mirage in front of me. Then, on the radio, Louis Armstrong came on with his rendition of *Wonderful World*. That was always her favorite song! She'd told me it gave her the hope she needed when she'd worked for the underground in World War II, while her island was occupied by German soldiers. As Louis Armstrong sang, I felt surrounded by warm, loving arms. "Moster Henny, I love you," I called out and stood up. I felt, more than heard, a gentle plunk of something falling from my lap. I looked down. It was the lost ring, Moster Henny's ring. The ring had been missing for quite sometime and had not been on my body. I reached down and put it on my finger as the song finished.

It truly is a wonderful world.

Michelle Porter shares her Newton, Massachusetts home with three very charming cats. After many years as a professional cook, she pursued a degree in Food Science & Nutrition. She currently offers personal nutritional counseling while pursuing her lifelong love of writing. Her short story, The Water Ghost of #35 *was published in* Haunted Encounters: Real-Life Stories of Supernatural Experiences *(Atriad Press, 2003, http://www.atriadpress.com). Michelle is also a volunteer reader for the Talking Information Center in Marshfield, Massachusetts, bringing the written word to the sight-disabled.*

Editor's Note: The Talking information Center (TIC) is a national link of radio and cable television stations offering their air space so volunteers like Michelle can read anything and everything in live and prerecorded broadcasts to the blind. Michelle does her readings at the offices of her local Boston newspapers. If you are interested in volunteering for this incredible organization, please see their website at http://www.ticnetwork.com/volunteer.html, or call them at (800) 696-9505.

28. It's Not What You've Been Taught to Believe
Tanya Olckers

My mother died suddenly in 2001. A heart attack claimed her at the age of 59. I quickly made arrangements to return to South Africa from the United Kingdom for her funeral, making my way through the wake of mourning with a sense of numbness and disbelief.

It was only after getting back to the UK that the full impact of her loss was felt. I took to asking her questions constantly. I firmly believe in life after death, and I hoped that wherever she was, she was able to hear me. My family has also had the strange talent of being able to see or talk to dead relatives, and somehow I hoped that she would be able to talk to me.

About six months after her death, I got my answer—my mom visited me in a dream, and I don't doubt for a moment that she came to me with the purpose of delivering a message.

In the dream, I saw her with my father, who was asleep in her arms. Upon seeing me, she left him and came to my side, leading me into a garden with an impossibly green lawn. It appeared to be a courtyard of sorts—very much like an old English university, with old stone buildings rising up all around us.

I asked her what she was doing there, that I thought she was dead. She told me that I wasn't mistaken, that she was, in fact, dead.

"So is this Heaven?" I asked.

"No," she answered, "This is where we all come to leave behind the things that we have brought back with us from the world. It's also where we come to talk to you who are still in the world. It's a halfway point where we can meet between your world and the next."

> *"(Heaven is) nothing like you may begin to imagine, nor is it anything like you have been taught to believe it is."*

"Well, if this isn't Heaven, then where is Heaven?" I wanted to know.

Mom pointed to a large glowing light at the corner of the courtyard. It was a mixture of gold and blue light, oval shaped, and it seemed to be pulsating. "It's just through there," she said.

"Have you seen it?" I asked.

"I have," she told me, "And it's nothing like you may begin to imagine, nor is it anything like you have been taught to believe it is."

She continued a brief conversation with me, which I no longer remember, after which I woke up finding that my cheeks were wet from crying.

I took this dream literally, knowing she had moved on to something beyond this world.

Mom's presence was not only felt in dreams. In June 2003, I had taken ill with a very high fever and was hospitalized for three days. After I had been hooked up to an IV and the nurse had left, my friend, Kate, stayed with me and held my hand, sitting at my left side. I also felt, very distinctly, the presence of my mother in the room, and she held my right hand. The pressure in my right hand was the exact pressure, texture, and warmth of a woman's hand, a woman who had held my hand countless times as a child when I was ill. Kate later told me that she constantly found herself looking up in the direction of where I felt my mother's presence, convinced that she would see a woman standing beside the bed, even though Kate and I were the only two people in the room.

Shortly after I returned home from the hospital, Mom visited me again in a dream.

I found her in the same courtyard this time. I didn't have to ask her anything. She simply turned to me and said, "Don't

think that where I am I don't feel emotion. I do miss you and it was difficult for me to leave your father after 40 years. But I am still with you. I was with you when you were in the hospital and I was with Dad when he had his heart attack."
And I know that she is still with me today.

Tanya Olckers has had several short stories published both online and in magazines in South Africa and the UK. She plies her trade as a freelance journalist over and above her day job. She currently lives in a small village with a friend and a cat in England.

29. Nona's Promise
Cheryl L. Stewart

I was born into a big, Italian Catholic family. The matriarch of our large family was my Nona, or "Nanita" (little grandmother), as many lovingly called her. My Nona was a tiny Sicilian woman with a sixth-grade education, a deep reverence for God, and an uncanny ability to foretell the future. Nona spoke in proverbs and in very broken English. She had a sweet, quiet, serene demeanor, and a powerful, loving energy about her presence that literally dominated a room. When Nona gave a gently warning like, "Don't go today. Go tomorrow," you waited until the next day to go wherever it was you had planned to go. Everyone in the family knew that to ignore her advice was a mistake; something would always go awry.

Nona was the eldest of four children and was only 15 years old when her mother died suddenly, leaving her to take care of her father and three younger siblings. Shortly after her mother's death, her father uprooted the family and immigrated to America, settling in Michigan. Her father saw America as the land of opportunity for Nona, but it was a very difficult time. Tasked with the responsibility of cooking, cleaning, finding a job, learning the language, and caring for her sister, Mary, and her two brothers, Alfred and Samuel (Alfred was an infant and Samuel still a toddler), my grandmother struggled to do it all. And all the while, she grieved for her mother.

In Italy, it was the custom to wear all-black attire when in mourning. My grandmother wore black every day for two years. When she was 17 years old, Nona's mother's voice awakened her, suddenly, in the middle of the night. She sat up in bed and, standing before her at the foot of her bed, shrouded in a bright white light, was her mother. Her mother said, "Take off your black. You have mourned too long. I am alive, in Heaven, healthy, and happy." My grandmother never wore black again.

When Loved Ones Return After Crossing Over

When I was a child, my grandmother and I used to wander through her gardens, picking fruits, vegetables, and beautiful flowers. We both loved flowers.

> *"Take off your black. You have mourned too long. I am alive..."*

During our times together, she would tell me many stories and, of course, the story of how her mother came to her to tell her that there was a Heaven, was one of them; the one most sacred to my Nona. She told it with such love and reverence that it left a deep and lasting impression on me.

Since she was raised as a Catholic, Nona prayed to a patron saint and, according to Nona, her patron talked with her regularly. When Nona was in her 60s, she developed diabetes, went blind, and became too ill to attend church. She used to say, "One does not need to go to church to talk to God. God is everywhere, in and through all things." These are the metaphysical beliefs I grew up on. "God is All That Is and all life is eternal. Our spirit never dies, but only sheds it's physical body and continues to live. So, we never lose anyone or anything." These beliefs saved my life.

I grew up in a difficult home environment and my Nona was my only source of love. Since my Nona was the only one who loved me and her home was the only safe and peaceful place I knew, I built my whole life on the beliefs she taught me. When I was 19 years old, Nona died. Before she died, I asked her, as I had asked as a child, if she would come back and see me like her mother had done for her, so that I would know that there was a Heaven. She touched my face lovingly and said, "Cheri, if there is a Heaven, I promise I will come back and tell you."

It took me two years and professional counseling before I could talk about Nona's death or really live my life. On my 40th birthday, I sat on the grass in my backyard in utter despair. My marriage had just ended, my teenage daughter was running wild, my finances were a disaster, and I felt like everything in

> "Our spirit never dies, but only sheds it's physical body and continues to live. So, we never lose anyone or anything."

my life was out of control. Nothing made any sense and I found myself questioning the validity of my faith and metaphysical beliefs for the first time in my life.

I looked at the heavens and called silently to my grandmother, "Maybe my whole life has been a lie because you didn't keep your promise and come back and talk to me. There must be no Heaven and no life after death. So when we die, we must lose everyone and everything we love and turn into nothing. This life is too painful, and I don't want to live knowing all I love will be forever lost. I don't believe there is a God anymore. If there were, you would have kept your promise. You didn't, so there must be nothing but loss."

My daughter, like my grandmother, had the ability to "see" and "hear" spirits, and even though she kept her gifts hidden, she would occasionally channel for me privately. At midnight one evening, my daughter, who had just returned home from a movie with her friends, came into my bedroom to kiss me goodnight. I was sleeping and her presence awakened me. Kissing my cheek, she said, "Happy Birthday. I'm sorry I wasn't here for your birthday. Oh, and someone wanted to talk to you, so I channeled for you and wrote the message down as a birthday present. I left it on the kitchen table. I think it was your grandmother."

Of course, I immediately sprang up out of bed to read the note my daughter had channeled. She never knew my grandmother or about her promise to me. She didn't know what a message from my beloved Nona meant to me, or that it was a promise being delivered after 21 years.

The note, a life-saving gift of love sent from the afterlife, written in my daughter's teenage scrawl and communicated to her through her spiritual guide, Grandfather, read:

> "There are two people here in my plane who were once on your earth with you. One wishes you to know she is with her love and they run together. She always wanted that, and she wanted you to know. She sends her cape of love and peace to you always."

(This was a message from an elderly woman who was my daughter's babysitter for six years. Her husband, who was an invalid, had died. She killed herself out of loneliness. I loved her and had always hoped that she would meet up with her husband. She did and wanted to tell me.)

The rest of the note was a message from my grandmother, fulfilling her promise to me 21 years after her death:

> "The other smiles upon your beautiful face and always watches over you with love and immense pride. She needs for you to know that she has kept her promise to you in her heart always. She carries out her promise in a different way; she can't give you understanding of why she must carry her promise out in a way you cannot see with your eyes. She wishes me to tell you that she sees deep down into your soul, and she knows you have not lost faith in her words, for she sees inside of you, her. She is explaining to me that I can't express all the love she has for you. She wants you to know that she has been, is, and always will be by your side, picking the flowers. She says, 'Know for me, Cheri.'"

Nona's message was worded in a way that I would recognize as "hers." To make it even clearer that the words were from her, she ended her message in broken English and she called me *Cheri*, a nickname that only she used: "*Know, for me, Cheri*," translates as "recognize that this is me." Say the words

> Her message from the afterlife is the most precious gift I have ever received.

aloud and you will hear the broken English—as my Nona spoke it. There was no doubt in my mind that this was my Nona sending a message to me, fulfilling a promise she made to me when I was a child.

This brief message from my grandmother may not seem like much to others, but the meanings in her message were completely understood by me. Her message from the afterlife is the most precious gift I have ever received. As I read her words, I felt her presence and realized that she couldn't come back and stand in front of me and talk with me, as her mother had done with her. The reason was that when she died, I had taken her death so hard that it nearly killed me. Feeling her loving energy and hearing her words through her message, I realized that I could not have endured seeing her again in any form because, when she again departed, I would feel like I was losing her a second time. I could not endure it, and I would be tempted to join her.

I knew these were not healthy feelings, and something she did not want. So she found a way to keep her promise in a way that would not make me feel like we were saying goodbye all over again. Instead, her channeled message, delivered through two other people (my daughter and her spirit guide) provided a way for her to keep her promise without re-igniting my grief.

Is there a Heaven, an afterlife where we go on eternally, still aware of and loving everyone and everything—where we never lose anyone or anything forever but, instead, just experience a temporary parting? My beautiful Nona traveled through time and beyond physical death, 21 years after her death, to keep her promise. I will never ask these questions again because, for me, they have been answered. We are all so blessed.

When Loved Ones Return After Crossing Over

Cheryl Stewart, a former vocational counselor who assisted disabled and injured individuals, is now a full-time freelance writer and editor. An avid reader, Cheryl began writing poetry when she was 11 years old. She continued to pursue her love of writing in high school where she became Feature Editor of her school newspaper, a member of the Scholastic Honors Society, and the recipient of numerous writing awards. She later majored in English journalism and art and earned an AA degree, several community poetry awards, and a BS degree in business and counseling psychology. Cheryl's writing and editing experience includes four years of advertising/marketing agency training and eight years as a freelance writer and editor. Today, she keeps herself busy editing books for new authors and writing grants, short stories, magazine articles, and marketing copy. Cheryl currently resides in Oceanside, California and enjoys the outdoors, outings with her large Italian family, metaphysics, and playing with her many beloved pets (a gander, two ducks, a Myna bird, a cat, and a dog).

30. She Implored Me Not to Be Sad
Suzanne Baran

Alicia befriended me about three years ago when we met through our mutual best friend, Jenny. The two attended law school in New York City together. Jenny and Alicia were both redheads, and I was the brunette of our triad. We became closer than sisters. We cried and laughed together. When I broke up with my boyfriend for the first time, they were there with wine and smiles, and they were the first ones to comfort me when my brother, Jeff, committed suicide. Every Saturday night, we went to our favorite hangout, American Trash, on the upper eastside. We played pool, flirted with the locals, and had philosophical talks in the ladies' room, sometimes until the sun came up.

Alicia was an expert pool player and had a hard life. She survived more tragedies, illnesses, and financial mishaps than anyone I've ever met, aside from my Holocaust survivor grandmother. In the two years I knew her, Alicia was diagnosed with Hepatitis C (which she hid from Julie and me until hospitalized). A man followed her into her building one night and sexually assaulted her. She narrowly escaped rape. Alicia was a full-time law school student at the age of 42 and plugged away at her studies while working as a transcriber for various editors and attorneys. She was poor and lived off disability insurance from her illness. A smile always colored her face, even when she worried about paying rent and feeding her four cats, and she was always charitable to those who had less than she did. I never saw her turn away an open homeless person's hand, and she always bought me drinks and showered me with love.

Five months after my brother killed himself, I received a call from Alicia's friend, Renee, informing me of her death. I sat stunned, unable to speak. I looked at the phone as a foreign object, dropped it, and screamed. The pain was too immense for my 25-year-old soul to bear. I'd been through the first stages of grief with my brother's death, and now I had to face losing Alicia. She was traveling in the Virgin Islands on some money she saved. She wanted to find a legal internship there for the summer and ride horses, while soaking in the sun and sand. Two days before her death, she sent me an email attachment with a picture of her sitting on a brown mare, wearing a wide smile. Things were working out well for her, she said. She seemed truly happy and worry-free for the first time since I met her. My heart was glad.

Details of her death were few. Apparently, she choked on something while alone in her room. Earlier that week, she'd lost the cell phone I gave her. When she didn't arrive at a party she'd been invited to, someone went looking for her. By the time help arrived, she was dead. It was a fluke accident, but it seemed to make sense to me. God took her when she was at her most fulfilled, her happiest, and she wasn't in pain any longer. Alicia was buried in the same cemetery as my brother, Jeff. She grew up in New York but the cemetery was in New Jersey, for some reason. I think God planned it this way so I could see them both at the same place. I kissed both their graves last summer in May.

Unfortunately, my life started to mirror Alicia's after she died. During her life, Alicia was riddled with mishaps, illness, disaster, and tragedy to the point where no one believed her when yet *another* bad thing happened to her. After Alicia died, I was laid off from work, broke up with my boyfriend of two years, moved out of three different apartments, ended a relationship with our mutual best friend, had an electrical fire in my room that wiped out hundreds of dollars of equipment, moved to Los Angeles, and experienced huge losses of money over bad roommates, decisions, and the like. I also moved into an unsafe neighborhood and was almost attacked, had my bankcard stolen, had a friend commandeer my job after I gave her work, got into a car accident and lost $1300, was

> She said she was happy now where she wasn't before, and she reprimanded me. She implored me not to be sad, to keep my head up, and dispel all melancholy surrounding her death.

hospitalized with tonsillitis twice, lost another job because I was too sick to work, got dumped by several men, and so on. On the night before what would be my car accident, Alicia appeared to me in a dream. I wrote it down on the morning of May 22nd of that year, the day I would be in a car accident and sustain minor physical injuries and major financial ones.

In the dream, Alicia told me my soul requested her. She led me to a grassy knoll, which was where I saw her new home. It was a tiny white cottage with white interior carpet, walls, and beds. Alicia was wearing all white, too. She said she was happy now where she wasn't before, and she reprimanded me. She implored me not to be sad, to keep my head up and dispel all melancholy surrounding her death. She doesn't want me to be sad, she said repeatedly and in her strong and familiar didactic tone. She loved Jenny, though they fought before her death, and she said she loved me. "We will go on," and "I will go on," she said, referring to herself. "I am irritated with your sadness and with you for being sad and dwelling on the past," she said.

My wreck was severe and my car was totaled. I think Alicia's warning was to prepare me for that and to teach me to be happy no matter what negativity was thrown my way.

In a dream sequence prior to this, I remember dreaming I was on a white sailboat. The deck was made of white painted wood. I walked to the helm of the boat and saw a brown mare, its mane blowing in the wind. I knew at that moment that Alicia was with me, surrounding me, giving me some sort of missive. The horse's name popped in my head, Amanda. I somehow knew her name. The sky was white. Then Alicia appeared from behind Amanda. I saw her long, red hair flowing as she petted her horse, and then the boat filled with water. Fish were floating in it, and I spotted a baby shark. I climbed up the ladder leading to the boat's stern and a huge dolphin tried snapping at me, but I somehow knew it wouldn't hurt me. It was goading me to get off the boat onto land, to live.

Suzanne Baran is a freelance journalist in search of a steady gig in Los Angeles, California, after leaving her financial journalism career in New York City.

31. "Mommy, I See Jack!"
Kim Davis

March 25, 1996 Journal Entry

"...With Jack so unwell, I have to admit that I'm just waiting for him to die. This clinging to life with drugs and constant pain and fear is so ugly. I just wish it would finish."

March 26, 1996 Journal Entry

"Oh what a day! Jack died at 10:00 a.m. Texas time. Mom's just called—all in pieces, obviously..."

My relationship with my stepfather, Jack (see photo 44 on page viii), was always strangely close. I remember the first time I met him when I was eight years old. It was as if I'd been waiting for him all my life. I clearly remember being irresistibly drawn to him, even though at that time both he and my mother were married to other people.

It was not until nearly four years later that I saw him again when he arrived to take my Mom on their first date. I clearly recall thinking "Oh, there you are. What took you so long?"

I can't imagine a more devoted husband for my mother. As a strong-willed woman who openly competed with men in business, Mom didn't find it easy to relate to men on a romantic level. She had always fit in better as "one of the boys." Jack, on the other hand, was the "strong, silent type," but with a difference. He had several special gifts, among them an eye for color and design, and an amazing ability to empathize with others. He was my mother's champion and protector for 24 years.

I wanted to do something special to let Jack know how much I cared for him, so I named my first child, Jacqueline, after him.

Little Jacqui, at the tender age of 27 months, accompanied me to Texas for Jack's funeral.

Mom was a basket case and stayed that way for much longer than I thought was healthy. Where she had been a strong, level-headed businesswoman before, without Jack, she found herself, for the first time in her life, a helpless woman in a man's world. She let her business suffer. I think she ate nothing but banana pudding for nearly a year. So, when she literally begged me, my husband, and daughter to come home for a vacation in September 1997, we couldn't refuse.

By this time, Jacqui was talking, and she talked quite a lot about Jack. I can recall driving along and having her shout "Mommy, I see Jack!" She did this often. One time, I was really amused when she was chattering away in the back seat. I couldn't quite hear her and then she told me, "I was talking to Jack." I now can't remember what she told me they were talking about, and neither can she. Sadly, Jacqui is eight years old now and says she doesn't remember her conversations or visits with Jack at all. It seems to me like only yesterday when she was telling me she saw Jack with wings guarding her in bed at night.

That visit with Mom led to us relocating to Texas from Spain. Our bedraggled little family arrived just in time for Thanksgiving, and the visits from Jack began to affect us all. We'd left nearly all our electronics in Europe and bought a new stereo, television, and computer when we got here, so it really caught our attention when the television and stereo began to turn themselves off and on. It was never scary, but it happened consistently enough to both my husband and myself that it was a topic of conversation. And from then on, we have gone through light bulbs at an alarming rate. We can't blame it on the wiring—we changed houses. We can't blame it on the lamps—it happens in all the light fixtures. We can't blame it on the light bulbs—we even bought the long-life bulbs. I think Jack's visiting.

> *"My work is almost done..."*

In the spring of 1999, just as the famous Texas wildflowers were blooming, I rejoined the workforce. My second daughter was just a year old. Everyday, as I drove past a particular field of bluebonnets, I felt like Jack was in the car and looking at the beautiful wildflowers with me. It was a road he'd traveled often in life, and I know he loved that spot. I'd mentally try to talk to him and, in response, I always got a sort of electrical charge, which I've come to think of as confirmation from the spirit world about whatever I happen to be thinking about.

Around that time, I had a dream in which I was with my mother and a new gentleman friend of hers. We went to see Jack, a fit, young Jack who seemed about 30 years of age. He invited us into his home. It was impeccably decorated, and there was a little dog. Jack took us out to see his new car and seemed very pleased with my mother's new fellow.

April 3, 1999 Journal Entry

"...'My work is almost done,' someone just told me. I don't think that implies an ending, but rather a beginning."

I was quite surprised when I wrote those words in my journal. I'd heard them clearly in my head, and it was just as clear that I did not think them. I knew it was Jack speaking to me. When the wildflowers finished blooming, I stopped having my visitor in the car on the way to work, and the odd electrical goings-on became less frequent as well.

What really clenched it for me was a conversation with my mother on the porch one Saturday shortly after that. Now you have to understand that Mom is not a person who ever had anything to do with anything metaphysical. She had, however, been reading about reincarnation. In particular, she told me that *Many Lives, Many Masters* by Brian Weiss brought her the most peace she'd found since Jack's passing.

On this particular Saturday, Mom and I had had a bit too much wine, a rare occurrence in our family, but the wine tasted good, and it was a day for talking. I'm not sure Mom would have told me about her conversations with Jack had we been sober.

She said, "I'm really pissed off at Jack," and I babbled a bit about that being a normal reaction to grief. But she said "No. I have been talking to him since he died, always out on my balcony where the table is. The other day he told me he's got to move on and do other things, and that I need to go on without him." Of course, the day coincided with my message to me about his work being finished.

The happy ending, if there ever is an "end" to any story, is that Mom has, indeed, moved on. Though it has taken her nearly seven years, she is once again the confident, outgoing woman Jack loved when he was alive. We all remember him, and we miss having him around to talk to, but his visits made it clear to us that we will see him again.

Kim Davis was brought up in the Bible Belt but, after studying the world's religions from the point of view of the philosophers at University, discovered a common thread connecting them all. Today, she meditates and loves her neighbors without the guidance of an organized religion. Kim also writes how-to books and articles and designs websites. Find out more at http://www.kpdavis.com.

32. We're Just on Different Sides of The Door
Paula Stahel

For once, a Bruce Willis movie was making a buzz for reasons other than bombs. In 1999, there were only two camps: Those who'd seen *The Sixth Sense* and those who hadn't. People who'd seen the movie wouldn't give away anything, but their eyes gleamed, and their voices took on a "just you wait" tension when they talked about it. Even my son was so impressed he went twice. "Mom," he told me, "you won't believe the ending!"

So I saw it. I liked it. Bruce Willis was pretty good. But the ending was so easy to foretell, I wondered what the big deal was. And I wondered why my own son thought I'd be surprised. He knows I see dead people.

The gift of sight has been with me since childhood. But if I was taught in church that this gift was evil, the lesson didn't take, probably because the very first time I encountered a spirit, it brought spiritual knowledge.

Memorizing the Lord's Prayer was a Sunday school assignment when I was six. I knew I was smart, but learning that prayer by heart seemed impossible. Every Sunday, more of the boys and girls in my class had it down pat, but I couldn't get past "thy will be done." My stomach tied itself in knots whenever I tried to recite it. Then one morning, on the way downstairs to breakfast, consumed with worry over learning the prayer, the face of a man appeared hovering just above and before me. I paused and waited. The man spoke: "Child, we are here to help you. We will teach you."

I wasn't scared, but I was surprised. There was no "we," there was only "he." I thought the man looked like God, but I knew it wasn't God. Just as quickly as he appeared, he was gone. I stood still for a moment, flawlessly reciting the Lord's Prayer.

When Loved Ones Return After Crossing Over

I never told anyone. I knew by then it was best to keep some secrets. My father got upset when I'd describe buildings coming up around corners in towns we'd never driven through before. My mom didn't like it when I'd tell her who was on the phone before she answered. I didn't like other people telling me things that were scary, so I didn't want to scare my mom and dad. I learned to keep things to myself.

Then, in my 30s, too many things, too many spirits, and too many messages started coming to me. Something new had begun, something I didn't fully understand.

The previous Christmas, I'd spent the holiday with family. On the day I left to return home, I stopped by my father's shop to say goodbye. When I hugged him, a sense—not of dread, but a tinge of foreboding—flowed through me with an impression of "heart" and "last goodbye." At my parent's home a while later, I hugged my mother, then my grandmother, Babi. The sense I'd felt earlier returned more strongly. I tried to put it out of my mind, without success.

Five months later, in the middle of an office meeting, a chill blew into the room. I was the only one who shivered. I turned to the door and glimpsed Babi for the shortest of seconds. Then, she and the chill were gone. I looked at the clock—it was a few minutes past three.

At home after work, the phone rang. I knew before answering it that it was my father. I knew before he finished saying hello that Babi had died. Her heart, he told me, just stopped, a few minutes past three.

There are many things that come to mind when I think of my grandmother. At the top of that list is buchti, a Czechoslovakian pastry. When Babi died, there was no one left who knew how to make it. I'd asked her once to teach me, but then I never went to visit so I could learn. I felt guilty about that. Now, I was determined to find a way to learn. I searched cookbooks for recipes similar to what I knew she did. I made batches of dough

> Why can't I get in touch with people whenever I want?"

and threw them out because they didn't seem right. Then one afternoon, something told me the dough *was* right. I started working it with my hands, not sure of what to do next. I heard Babi speak into my ear. She was standing just behind my left shoulder. "No, no," she said, "pinch off just a little bit. Now roll the ball lightly. Good. Now pat it in your hand. No, not palms together, pat with your fingertips...."

I made pans full of buchti, wrapped them carefully, and sent them as surprises to my parents and my two brothers. When each told me, "They taste just like Babi made them!" I wanted to say, "She did!"

Babi wasn't the only one who'd passed on and was now visiting me. So many of them were people I didn't know. Needing to understand more, I headed to the parapsychology stacks at the library.

Being the kind of person who straightens pictures in other people's houses, I absentmindedly pushed in a book sticking out from the shelf. I'd choose a book, glance through it, put it back, choose another. The same book I'd pushed in was sticking out again. Odd—but, oh well, maybe I'd dislodged it while getting another nearby. I pushed it back in once more. I looked through a few more, and then saw the book again. This time, it was tilted forward, perilously close to falling from the shelf. Startled, I realized the book was choosing me! I pulled it down and looked at the title: *No Good-Byes: My Search into Life Beyond Death* by Adela Rogers St. Johns, the writer who had created the sob-sister genre for William Randolph Hearst, and a woman I'd admired for years. She had written about her search for healing after the devastating loss of her son, Bill. I was on my way to finding answers, at least some.

There are still more questions than answers. One of them is "Why can't I get in touch with people whenever I want?" Maybe we're not supposed to. Maybe they'd never get any of their own work done if we constantly dropped in like neighbors announcing, "I've come to visit!" I know I'd be knocking way too often at one particular door.

> We grieve for ourselves more than for the one we've lost.

Just before my 20th high school reunion, my family held its own reunion. For the first time since I'd graduated, all of us gathered at our old family resort. I was divorced and attended with my 10-year-old son. My younger brother had his wife and five kids along. My youngest brother, Mike, was newly wed to Kelli, whose 21st birthday we celebrated with a cookout at the lakeshore.

The day before I left, as I lounged near the water, a screen door slammed. I turned my head to watch Mike stride from his cottage. At the same moment, my father strolled past me along the sand. Suddenly, that sense was with me again, the sense I'd felt months before Babi died. I knew instantly that never again would we all be together in that special place. Someone would be gone from the picture before we could all return but I didn't know who it was.

The answer didn't come as quickly this time. Two years and 11 months later, Mike died of Hodgkin's disease. He and Kelli had become parents to a son, Josh, 10 months before.

There is no passing that does not devastate a family. We grieve for ourselves more than for the one we've lost. We slowly healed as best we could. In morning meditations, I always let Mike know I was there if he needed to share anything. Occasionally, he did. I did most of the sharing, much of which was focused on how angry I was that he hadn't had the decency to leave a forwarding address so I could write him, so I could stay in touch. He reminded me that I already did.

A few years went by. Kelli fell in love with a man who adored my nephew. My father was happy for Pete and Kelli, my mother thrilled. Years before, Pete had been a student at the junior high where my mother had been a secretary. His mother was a

> None of them are gone, no more than my husband is when he's in another room. We're all still here, just on different sides of the door.

friend of hers. They married and wanted children. Within months, Kelli was pregnant. Within weeks, she lost the baby.

Again, we hurt. But something else gnawed at me. One day, I sat meditating and specifically sought out Mike. When I saw him, he was standing at a workbench concentrating on a project, not overjoyed at my interruption.

"Mike," I said, "What happened to the baby?"

"Pete needs to have more time with Josh first. There'll be another."

"Another baby?"

"Yes. She'll be pregnant within a year." He turned away, went back to his work, and vanished.

Kelli had her second son 18 months later.

The longer Mike's gone, the less he comes around. I guess his work, whatever it is, keeps him busy. But he contacts us occasionally. He telephoned my mother one evening—she's certain; my father's not so sure. The Christmas my son was a high school freshman, playing the saxophone in the band, an unusually large, heavy gift arrived for him from Kelli. Inside was Mike's alto sax. Through tears over the phone, she said Mike had been visiting her for weeks, telling her he wanted her to send it.

Then one of our other brother's sons married. I chose a selection of cooking utensils as their gift, but could find nothing just right to hold the beautiful olivewood spoons and whisks. It was Mike who came up with the solution: He told me clearly that I was to put them in the blue pottery pitcher he'd made in college and specifically say that part of the gift was from him. I did, even though everyone in the room dissolved into tears when gifts were opened and the card was read. My nephew sobbed on my shoulder, thanking me over and over for letting him know his uncle Mike was with us.

And he still is. So are my grandparents, and dozens of other family and friends who've gone ahead—VanDercar, who I found standing at the foot of my bed one night the year after he passed; the grandmother of my son's high school girlfriend, giving me a message to pass along; a close friend of my mother's wanting her children to know she was watching over them. The list goes on. Forever.

So do we all. None of them are gone, no more than my husband is when he's in another room. We're all still here, just on different sides of the door.

Paula Stahel is an author and personal historian in Tampa, Florida. Her most recently published work is Ted Hull's memoir, The Wonder Years: My Life and Times With Stevie Wonder, *published by Booklocker.com. As a professional, personal historian, she writes and privately publishes people's life stories as family legacies, conducts seminars, and teaches life-story writing classes. Her essays have appeared in the* St. Petersburg Times *and the* Christian Science Monitor.

33. Bye, Bye, Charlie
Jim Murray

Excerpted from Good Time Charlie, *a work in progress by Jim Murray.*

The man at the front door was simply huge! I can still see his gigantic form in my mind's eye, despite the passage of more than 50 years. I recall his broad smile, his double chin, and his jet-black hair, slicked straight back against his massive skull. But most of all, I remember the large black tool bag that he toted.

"Hello, Jimmy, is your grandma home? I'm here to fix her TV set."

"How do you know my name?" I asked. "Who are you?"

"I'm your Uncle Charlie," the smiling 6-foot giant proclaimed as he stepped into the vestibule (see photo 17 on page vi).

"You are?"

Charlie roared with laughter. I led the stranger up the front stairs into my grandmother's living room and watched with fascination as he began to disassemble the 1950 vintage RCA television. Apparently, my grandmother was in no hurry to make an appearance.

The repairman dug down into his magic bag. He produced wonderful tools with colorful plastic handles. He brought forth strange electronic meters with flashing lights and mysterious dials and fluorescent discharge probes, which drew long crackling electric arcs from the tops of various vacuum tubes in the TV's high voltage chassis.

By the time Granny did enter the room, repairs were nearly complete and the big man was already packing up his electrical treasures. I watched with great longing as each instrument and tool disappeared back into the black carrying case. Desperately, I wanted such things for my own. Even at the tender age of four, I could envision myself making use of them.

Finally, in desperation, I extended my little hand, gently patted the bag, and petitioned the unusual visitor, "Do you think that you could leave these here so I can try them out, too?" I pleaded.

The jolly giant burst out laughing, but before he could reply to my question, Grandma interjected,

"Charlie is a very busy man, Jimmy. He needs his tools to do his work. Don't be bothering him!"

Sadly, I watched the giant visitor depart. But I could never forget him. That brief exposure to the art of TV repair had a profound effect on me as a youngster. In fact, I have often wondered if old Charlie might not have been responsible for me becoming an electrical engineer.

Charlie B., what a character! He was one of those rare individuals who exploded into the world from obscure origins, but left an enormous impact on all those he encountered. He most assuredly left his mark on old Jersey City. His stories and antics will live on forever in the minds and hearts of those who loved him. He was acquainted with four generations of Murrays, but his greatest impact will probably be felt by my children, the current generation.

Charlie was born and raised in western Pennsylvania. He spoke little of his childhood, but made it clear that times were tough while he was growing up. He left home at a very young age and haphazardly migrated to Chicago where he received his degree in street smarts. Ultimately, he began to wander eastward again and, eventually, wound up in the Bronx at the tender age of 12.

Mr. B. had a prodigious intellect and so many interests that he was often beside himself. Personally, I believe he was an "Indigo Child" but, Indigo or not, one fact stands out loud and clear; Charlie was a true renaissance man, and he was self made. However, like others of his kind, he just couldn't remain focused on any one career.

During his youth, he studied voice, language, and opera, and was actually coached, from time to time, by Enrico Caruso in New York City. As his talents developed, he sang in various churches, entertained the rich and famous, and even cut records of his own voice at the Metropolitan Opera House.

However, all was not culture and class! Charlie had to eat, too and, during the depression, that was not always easy to accomplish. Applying a customized mix of street smarts and entrepreneurial skills, the young runaway started a battery charging business in the basement of a Bronx funeral home. Apparently, the proprietor also paid Charlie to live in a small cellar apartment so that "the bodies would not be left unattended."

With monies so earned, Mr. B. eventually attended a class on motion picture technology and became aggressively interested in "talkies," or talking pictures, as they were called back then. The Radio Corporation of America held the patents on film sound track detection and amplification equipment, and it wasn't long before my old friend was lured into the emerging field of electronics.

Initially, he studied electrical engineering and radio design. Charlie operated one of the first commercial radio stations in the state of New Jersey. But his talents did not go unnoticed by Uncle Sam. During the war, he was put in charge of the installation and maintenance of early forms of radar and gun positioning equipment for the United States Navy's Atlantic Fleet.

Sometime after the war, Charlie went to work for Ma Bell during the day and became involved in the restaurant business at night. He had two partners, Pete and Dominic, and the enterprise became a real landmark in Jersey City. The "club" attracted all sorts of interesting clientele, including politicians and mobsters from New York City and many surrounding towns. The place was always jumping.

I suppose that it was inevitable, but Charlie B. just couldn't resist the lure of politics. Through his connections at the club, he was introduced to all the right people and, before long, he was invited to campaign for mayor LaGuardia in New York City and, later, for the Victory Ticket in Jersey City. However, despite his enthusiasm, he personally never held public office.

Charlie went west for several years during the mid-50s and engaged in mining, timber reclamation, and other exploits. However, he returned to Jersey City sometime in the early 60s and promptly invested in real estate. He secured equity in a large apartment complex and began to manage the property. It was there that we finally became reacquainted. Charlie generously provided me with room and board while I attended college.

This new association allowed me to spend countless hours visiting with my old friend. As our relationship grew, Charlie shared more and more stories with me. It was impossible to get bored. All of his adventures seemed larger than life and, though many of his deeds may have been exaggerated, there was no doubt that the basic tales were absolutely true. Far too many photographs, magazine articles, and old associates existed to support his claims. Often, I was mesmerized for hours.

Charlie's adventurous tales and the reports of his exploits filled me with a sense of wonder and inspiration. I had great hopes of becoming as accomplished and wealthy as this multi-talented individual. Yet, as I got to know him better, there were subtle hints that old Charlie was more than just a man of the world. There was a mystical and spiritual side to this remarkable person. However, this more sensitive component was usually kept locked up deep inside his being.

This nonmaterial side of his nature would rupture forth every now and then, usually when he sang along with recordings of Caruso, Geilie, or Thomas. Sometimes, a hint of his hidden self might be detected when he reminisced about his childhood and his mother. But his secret side became most obvious when he opened himself up to the innocence of little children.

REAL STORIES OF SPIRIT COMMUNICATION

> "...that's not what God had in mind at all."

Often, Charlie would baby sit for his tenants or their guests. He loved to entertain young kids. His favorite game was to perform as a magician. Most often, he announced himself as "The Great Hezekiah" and proceeded to execute all manner of tricks and prestidigitation. He also sang songs, played the ukulele, and produced remarkable animal imitations, all for the delight of the little ones. His dedication to this end seemed utterly complete; his energy boundless.

"Say Charlie," I asked one day, "You really love kids, don't you?"

"Oh sure, Jimmy Pal, but it's way more than that!"

"What do you mean?"

"Well, little children are still plugged into the bosom of God. They have not yet been blinded by the folly of man. Hence, they can see only truth, and they speak only truth, directly from the heart. That's where we get the age old saying, 'Truth shall flow from the mouths of babes.'"

But once the "little people" were gone, old Charlie would collapse into his big easy chair and brood. Originally, I thought it was because he had no family of his own, and he was plagued with loneliness. But, eventually, I learned otherwise.

"You know, Jimmy, the world will turn those little darlings into absolute monsters someday, and that's not what God had in mind at all! It's a cruel, unfair existence out there, I know."

Sometimes Mr. B. would let other secrets slip out of the bag if his mood was somber enough.

"Jimmy Pal, there's more to life than meets the eye, and death is just a joke. Remember what I tell ya, my friend, and someday you'll understand!"

I never knew how to take such tutoring. Was it just the rambling of an eccentric old man, or was Charlie B. a mystic among so many other things? He once confided a story to me that gave me great cause to wonder.

"I was playing on the lawn in front of the house one day when I was a very young boy. I wasn't feeling too well. I think I was getting over bronchitis or something. My mother was hanging out the wash. All at once, a fierce wind began to blow right out of a clear, calm spring sky. Then, suddenly, a huge tent appeared on the lawn, as if by magic! Mother was terrified! I picked up a big piece of firewood and ran over to protect her. But then the tent opened and out stepped an A-rab, all decked out, complete with a big turban, gold chains, and jewels.

"The guy smiled at me and motioned me over to the tent. Somehow, I knew he was okay, so I dropped my club and wandered over there. He showed me all around inside his place. It was full of old books, big steamer trunks, and lots of colored bottles filled with all kinds of stuff. I didn't understand most of what he told me. But then he brought me back over to my mother and kinda examined me all over. He rubbed his fingers through my hair like he was massaging my scalp. Then put his hands flat upon my head. He looked up at the sky and moved his lips in silence. I think he was praying or something.

"Then the A-rab smiled again and said to my mother, 'Don't worry, the boy will be all right.' Then he went back into the tent, closed the flap, and whoosh, the tent blows away. I never saw that A-rab guy again, but he was right about what he told my ma. Everything turned out just fine. I think the guy was some kind of angel, Jimmy, and, someday, I might see him again. You know, at the very end."

Charlie was in his 70s when I finally got married, but our friendship never wavered. When he entered the old age home in Jersey City, plagued with poor health, I visited him often and I brought him home on weekends for hot meals and family affection. By the time our daughter, Kelly, was born, Charlie was spending a great deal of time in a wheelchair. His prodigious weight and many years of inactivity had taken a drastic toll on his muscles and joints. But his spirits never atrophied, and neither did his humor.

REAL STORIES OF SPIRIT COMMUNICATION

When my daughter was two years old, I began taking her up to the hospital to visit my dear old friend. She was like a ray of sunshine in that dingy ward and Charlie really brightened up when he saw her. Kelly would bring him little gifts, and he would give her trinkets, love notes, and cookies in return. They became good pals. My only regret was that my baby would never know the Charlie that I had known, the musical genius of Jersey City, the animal impressionist, the Great Hezekiah!

The birth of my son, James, was a great event for the family, but also for Mr. B. My wife and I had him down to the house many times to visit with the new arrival. Whenever Charlie would hold my infant boy in his arms, his old blue eyes would fill with tears.

"Jimmy," he announced one day, "This is the fourth generation of Murrays that I have known and loved. I knew you when you were just this little, too. My God, what a feeling. You have filled my life with joy, pal, and I'll never forget you."

The following spring, I took the family on an outing to Lancaster County, Pennsylvania. We visited the railroad museum in Strasburg and took a steam train ride all the way up to the town of Paradise. Then we visited various shops, museums, and restaurants. The entire family had a wonderful time. Even young James, who was stroller-bound at the time, seemed to have fun. By the time we got home, the sun was just setting and everyone was tired.

Little Kelly ran down the hallway to her bedroom to undress while my wife struggled with James. I got the family dog ready for a well-deserved walk. Suddenly, the telephone rang. I grabbed the receiver. It was Charlie's brother. I could tell immediately from the tone of his voice that something was very wrong.

"Mr. Murray, I regret to inform you that my brother died about an hour ago. I know that you were very close to him; I'm terribly sorry."

I put down the phone in absolute shock. A million things were suddenly running through my head. But, strangely, my greatest concern was for little Kelly's reaction to the loss. I dashed down the hallway to find her. Her bedroom was empty. I crossed the hall and checked our bedroom. There she was. My little girl was lying on the left side of our bed, propped up by a pile of pillows, and still clad in her coat and hat.

Kelly displayed a radiant smile. She was looking up at the ceiling and waving her little hand enthusiastically.

"Bye, bye, Charlie," she said softly, "Goodbye, Uncle Charlie."

I starred at the vacant ceiling, filled with wonder.

"How could she possibly know?" I thought, "I just found out myself!"

Gently, I took my little daughter in my arms and held her. I looked into her big blue eyes. They were clear and bright and she was not upset at all.

"Darling," I said softly, "Charlie is dead."

"I know, Daddy, I was saying goodbye to him." She looked skyward again. "Bye, bye, Charlie," she concluded still smiling. "Charlie is happy now, Daddy."

Suddenly, I could hear my old friend's words echoing through my mind,

"Truth shall flow from the mouths of babes."

I hugged my little girl, knowing full well that she could tell only the truth.

"Bye, bye Charlie," I repeated, and I began to cry.

Jim Murray was born and raised in Jersey City, New Jersey. He is the son of the late Senator James F. Murray, Jr. and grandson of the late Commissioner James F. Murray, Sr. He is an engineer, researcher, and writer presently living in Piscataway, New Jersey. He is also the author of the soon to be released book, Tunnels, *an autobiographical account of the death defying adventures of two young boys on the Jersey City railroads and surrounding terrain. Additional information may* be obtained by sending an email to Jim Murray at JFMIII152h@hotmail.com.

Editor's Note: You can read more about Indigo Children at http://www.indigochild.com.

34. The Reason I Came to This Earth
Sabrina Zackery

This is dedicated to the memory of my father, who left this earth plane when I was four, but never left my side.

I was on a journey; a journey of self-discovery. I was born and raised Catholic, but my religion did not have the answers. I was the oldest of three girls and took my job of being the eldest seriously. I had led a very sheltered and strict existence. Now it was time for a change.

I had great time trying to find myself. I also had a great job and a great apartment. My high-visibility position in the entertainment industry led me to all the 'A' list parties. I attended movie premieres and restaurant openings. I even attended the Emmys. I drank, I smoked, and I partied in the fast lane. And the men—any age, size, or shape—were everywhere. Was this the real me, or was I making up for lost time?

Then it all stopped. Several events took place within a 7-day period that changed my life forever. I had been jockeying for a new position at my job. The position would give me a big raise and bounce me into upper management. I schmoozed the right people and appeared at the right parties. I was ready for the biggest career move of my life. I got the nod from my boss to hire my staff. I submitted a list of perfect candidates. I arranged interviews and videoconferences for candidates out of town. I narrowed down my list and drafted a budget for my department. Then it happened.

My boss balked at my choice of candidates. She returned my budget proposal slashed by 50%. She answered my memo with her own, stating her choices of who *my* staff would be. When I tried to confront her, she evaded every question. I was

> I listened to him say how he never left my side for all these years, how every time I wondered if I were making the right decision, he would show me a sign. I listened to him say how peaceful it was on the other side...

angry, then upset. But most of all, I was hurt. Nevertheless, I behaved like a good little Catholic girl and took it all in stride.

Then I experienced another blow. My beautiful apartment was going condominium. A corporate conglomerate had purchased the building once owned by an elderly couple. I had 90 days to decide to buy. But I was lucky. I could get it for a steal. I could purchase my closet apartment for a mere $350,000.

I did not have a dime to my name. All my credit cards were maxed-out. And a savings account? Forget about it. When I turned to my family for help, I got no sympathy.

I was stuck. I was alone. My God had forsaken me because I had been a 'bad' girl. All that time spent building a career, making a home for myself, and for what? It was all fading away.

It was dusk. I sat in the living room trying to make sense of it all. My body was lifeless. The air was heavy and warm. I couldn't breathe. Then I felt something. Coolness filled the room. I glanced at the window, but it was closed. Then I felt something else. I turned.

There he stood, a young waif of a man with a glowing smile, just like in the picture. I knew this man. This was my father (see photos 22 and 23 on page vi).

A flush of peace came to me. I sat transfixed. Then he spoke, and I listened. I listened to him say how he never left my side for all these years, how every time I wondered if I were making the right decision, he would show me a sign. I listened to him say how peaceful it was on the other side. I listened to him say how much he had learned by leaving this earth. But what I didn't want to hear was that he had to go. Our time

together was over, and he had to move on to yet a higher dimension. But he promised me that I would have other teachers to take his place. He said, "You are the reason I came to this earth. I am proud to be your father."
And then he was gone.

My life changed that day. It all made sense from that moment on. I left the big city to pursue my passions and to write.
Every time I pick up my father's golf clubs, I know exactly where that ball is going when I swing. Is that my golf instructor's voice in my head or my father speaking to me?
Every time I put my foot in a stirrup and compete with my horse, I know exactly how to approach the jump and clear it. Is that my riding instructor coaching me through the course, or is it my father guiding me to a clear round?
Every time I dance a waltz, I feel my instructor guide me across the dance floor like an angel. Or is it my father dancing with me?
My father was passionate about golf, horses, and dance. My instructors fuel the same passion in me. And, sometimes, when I close my eyes, I feel my father when I dance, ride, and golf. And I'm proud to be his daughter.

Sabrina Zackery, an award winning writer and photographer, left Los Angeles, California 12 years ago to pursue her passions. Her favorite is writing. Her most recent script, Change Partners, *has been named as a finalist in the* American Gem Scriptwriting Contest. *The script is based on Sabrina's experiences as a ballroom dancer. Currently, Sabrina is revising her first script,* The Horse of His Dreams, *which is based on the life of Joseph Donohue, a professional horse trainer. Mr. Donohue was featured in* Stories From The Sagebrush, *published by the University of Nevada, Reno and is known across the country for his alternative and holistic methods of healing horses. A dream led him to Reno, Nevada where he single handedly captured a runaway mustang* stallion. You can contact Sabrina Zackery at zacksplace123@hotmail.com.

35. You Must Go Visit Your Grandmother
Jennifer Grisdale Krieger

They say there's nothing more important than the Gift of Life, but what about the gift of helping a loved one crossover into a new life, perhaps even easing the transition from this world into the next?

I was able to give that gift, as was my mother (see photo 6 on page vi), although neither one of us realized the significance of what we were doing at the time. Here are our stories.

"I need your help!" That's how my dream started. It was the spring of 1984 and, while I'd had dreams before where he'd visited me, I had never experienced anything quite like this.

My grandfather, my father's father, the man we called "Dandad" (see photo 32 on page viii), had been dead for over a decade when I had this particular dream. He stood in front of me, wearing his favorite maroon velvet smoking jacket and smoking his trademark pipe, his brown eyes anxious behind his horn-rimmed glasses. "Jennifer, I need your help," he said again. "You must go visit your grandmother. She cannot be released until you do. Promise me you'll go visit her as soon as you can." Dandad's voice was gentle, but firm; a tone of voice I knew well. You didn't argue with that voice.

"Of course I will, Dandad!" I could hear myself saying the words aloud, as I woke up, startled. My new husband stirred, but remained asleep beside me. Our bedroom, dimly visible in the early dawn light, revealed nothing out of the ordinary. I slipped out of bed, pulled on my bathrobe, and padded down the hallway toward the stairs to the kitchen, our black cocker spaniel, Bosco, dutifully following me. I needed to think. And to think at that hour, I needed coffee.

> "You must go visit your grandmother. She cannot be released until you do."

Then, as a young woman in my mid-20s, I knew next to nothing about paranormal experiences of any kind. I knew that since my beloved Dandad had died from a massive stroke when I was 15, I had dreamt about him several times and had sensed his presence. I had drawn great comfort from those experiences. He and his wife, my grandmother, Nang (see photo 33 on page viii), had been the center of my world during my childhood. All holidays were spent at Nang and Dandad's Cape-style home in Weymouth, Massachusetts. Nang taught me how to bake, while sharing amusing snippets about her childhood in Lancashire, England. Her voice, with that lilting accent, a lovely mixture of British chipperishness and Scottish brogue peculiar to those raised in northern England, rose slightly when she became animated. Dandad and I, on the other hand, would have more serious conversations on a variety of topics.

After Dandad died, Nang was never the same. Eventually, she became very ill and disoriented, not recognizing her family or friends. Finally, she slipped into a coma. Nang had been comatose for many months when I had that dream. Although we visited her regularly, she never gave us any sign that she knew we were there.

So, several cups of coffee later, as I began to fully appreciate the clarity and intensity of my dream, I decided the right thing to do was to act upon my grandfather's request.

It was a warm, early June morning as my Mom (in whom I had confided) and I made our way to the now defunct Long Island Chronic Care Hospital located on Long Island in Boston Harbor. Nang's room was at the end of a short hall, and I can still remember the sound of my footsteps echoing down the narrow hallway. Nang's room was large and bright, a rather determined light, I had often thought, against the impending shadow of death.

When Loved Ones Return After Crossing Over

Imagine our amazement when, as my Mom and I entered this room, we found Nang awake! And not only that, but chatting with the nurses! Shortly before we arrived, she'd simply awakened, as if from a sound sleep. Nang recognized us immediately and, while her voice was rather hoarse, the lilting accent was still there. She was eager to hear all the latest news, and so we filled her in about my recent wedding and other family events. When Nang grew tired, my Mom and I hugged her close and said our good-byes. As I walked back down that hall, I turned and looked at Nang. She waved to me, and I waved back, blowing kisses. Shortly after we left, Nang slipped back into her coma.

Several nights later, I had another dream. This time, I was standing at the foot of the stairs in my parents' home. Walking slowly down the stairs toward me were my Dandad and Nang, arm-in-arm. He was still in his smoking jacket; she was wearing a favorite purple and blue dress with a bright red belt. Her hair was neatly coifed in her preferred style. Both were smiling happily at me. When they reached the bottom step, they hugged me tightly, the warmth of their bodies penetrating deeply into my bones. I abruptly woke up.

I was crying when I awakened, but they were happy tears. And it wasn't long before my Mom called to tell me what I already knew: Nang had, indeed, crossed over.

Jennifer Grisdale Krieger's work has appeared in a number of publications around New England including The Boston Globe *and* Boston Herald. *She lives with her husband, two sons, and a variety of critters in Northwest Massachusetts.*

36. This Is As Far As I Can Go With You
Jennifer Grisdale Krieger

Although my Mom's voice broke while recently retelling the story, the sense of awe and privilege she felt at being allowed to share this exceptional moment with her own mother, whom her grandchildren called Mama Nana (see photo 43 on page viii), was apparent.

"I had a super relationship with my mother," my mother explained. "She was a good friend, as well as being my mother. It's like that song, *I Still See Elisa,* from the musical, *Paint Your Wagon.* When you thought of her, you always thought of love."

So, in retrospect, as Mama Nana lay critically ill and unconscious on the last day of January 1977, it seemed quite natural that she should invite my Mom to join her on one last trip.

"I was sitting by her bedside," Mom recounted, "and I just closed my eyes for some reason. I began to feel dizzy. I said to my mother, with my eyes still closed, 'I feel dizzy!'

In my mind, she said back to me, 'I feel dizzy, too. Let's hold hands; maybe that will help.'"

As Mom grasped Mama Nana's hand, she felt the dizziness increase. Suddenly, they began falling down a tunnel.

"We began tumbling over and over and over," Mom continued, "and then we landed with a little thump at the bottom of this tunnel-like affair." Ahead of them was daylight, an opening in the tunnel. Mom peered through that opening, marveling at what she saw. "I could see a walkway going around the base of a mountain. I saw a lot of greenery and rocks. And at the end of this walkway stood my grandfather, my father, and some other people that I knew. I said to my Mother, 'Grampy [my Mom's grandfather] is waiting for you.'

She answered, 'Yes.'

Then I said, '*This is as far as I can go with you.*'

And my Mother said to me, *'Yes, dear, I know.'*

"And I just opened my eyes." My Mom found herself still in the hospital room with Mama Nana still unconscious in the bed beside her.

Mama Nana's kind heart stopped beating a short time later. She never regained consciousness, but she didn't need to. My Mom already knew her beloved mother was safe.

Jennifer Grisdale Krieger's bio appears in the preceding chapter.

37. I Told You So
Diana Thistle Tremblay

My father, Mel Thistle (see photo 40 on page viii), and I had an ongoing argument for the last 20 years of his life. He insisted that our consciousness ends with our death. I disagreed.

When I lived at home during university, we used to sit in his den and talk about the nature of life. Often, our discussion extended to the nature of death as well. When we'd get to the critical point in the discussion, I'd say, "I'm sorry, Dad, but I just know there's a life after death." And we would agree to disagree, but it troubled me. I couldn't understand how someone who wrote poetry and read philosophy could insist that this one physical life is all there is.

Finally, I got up the courage to challenge him on it. "Dad," I ventured, "Since we don't agree on this, maybe whichever of us dies first can come back and tell the other one."

"Well, I'll probably go first," he replied. "I'll come back and tell you, 'See, I told you there was no such thing as an afterlife.'"

We both laughed. After that, whenever we discussed life after death, we repeated our joke and laughed again. I knew he still didn't believe me, but he had made me a promise, joking and disbelieving, but a promise nonetheless. I was satisfied.

Sure enough, my father went first, at the age of 80. There was a solar eclipse on the day of his funeral. As sad as I was, the eclipse made me smile. I thought it was good timing on Dad's part. I longed to tease him about it.

I missed him terribly. I missed our talks. I missed our jokes. I kept thinking, "Oh, I must tell Dad about that," and then I'd remember that he was gone.

Six months after Dad died, I attended a spiritualist church service. Toward the end of the service, the minister shared messages she had from people's loved ones who had passed on. She came to me.

"I have a gentleman here," she said. "He feels like a father. He's wearing a carnation in his lapel. Can you accept him?"

My father used to wear a carnation on fancy occasions to distract from the absence of a tie, which he refused to wear when he got older. "Yes, thank you," I replied to the minister. She continued, "He came in calling something like 'Sweetie, Sweetie,' and I had to ask him who 'Sweetie' is."

The minister paused a moment, then added, "He seems like quite a jovial fellow. He doesn't have much to say right now. He says he's coming to you at this time because he said he would."

I thanked the minister and sat there stunned for the rest of the service. Dad had fulfilled his promise to me. He had reported back from the afterlife. Part of me wanted to jump up and grin and say, "I told you so, Dad!" But another part of me just sat there thinking, "Wow. There really is an afterlife!" As certain as I'd thought I had been, there had still been some doubt.

It took me until the next day to recall what "Sweetie" was all about. It wasn't a term of endearment that my father used. Then I remembered what he would call me when he meant to get my attention gently, especially if he needed to wake me: "Sweetheart!"

Now I am sure that our consciousness does indeed continue after our death. I'm also sure that my father is doing just fine. And I don't need to miss him so terribly. Someday, we'll meet up again. When we do, I'll bet he'll say, "See? I told you there was no such thing as an afterlife!"

One day, as I was helping my mother prepare the family home for sale, I smelled my dad's aftershave so strongly in his old den that I went to check the nearby bathroom to see if my mom had spilt a bottle of it. There was no scent in there and, when I returned to the den, the smell was gone.

I returned to the same church and the same medium was there. My dad came through again and asked if I'd been "tipping through" his books. The message I received was to look carefully, and I would find something I could "use right now."

The minister/medium said that my dad had been quite precise about the words "tipping through" his books. I knew what he meant; going through books on a bookshelf, tipping each one out on its corner, then tipping it back in.

I thought, at first, that my father meant for me to find a particular book while I finished my task of packing up the den. The den was a little room tucked in by the stairs. It was mostly taken up with a huge cherry wood desk that my dad built himself to fit in that space. Beside the door was a bookshelf, and beside that, a single bed tucked underneath a heating duct from the furnace.

I started with the bedside bookshelf. I marked a box for myself and put a number of interesting books aside. The rest I boxed for sale to a nearby second-hand bookshop. I rescued all the science fiction, and the others I chose were mostly about metaphysics. I was surprised by the depth of my father's reading in this area. Did he actually read the *Tibetan Book of the Dead*, for example?

Next, I tackled the wall bookshelves around the desk. I found that "tipping out" the first book revealed one of several boxed sets of coins that were hidden there. I showed the coins to my mom. I had already told her what the medium said, and my mother thought that I should keep the coins as mine.

They weren't very valuable, a few hundred dollars, but it was certainly something that I could use "right now."

I continued to attend that church periodically. My paternal grandmother, Nanny, came through, identifying herself the first time by her passionate interest in needlework and her frustration with her arthritis later in life, which prevented her from continuing her hobby through her later years.

When Loved Ones Return After Crossing Over

My maternal grandmother came through once, but only to say that she regretted not having appreciated me during her lifetime, which she certainly didn't. I don't think she liked children, or fun, or my father, or anybody much except sour old Mrs. Clermont, our part-time housekeeper and babysitter.

It was nine years ago that my father passed away. I seldom attend church now but I still go back to the same church at least every two years or so. I know if there will be a message for me that day—and there isn't always—because I'll feel a chill in my back. Sometimes, I feel that chill in my back at home and, some of those times, I sense it's my father. I don't know how to receive specific communications from him, so I just stop and think of him kindly and surrounded by light.

Diana Thistle Tremblay is a freelance writer who writes mostly for children, both fiction and nonfiction. Her father, Mel Thistle, was a journalism professor. His books included Peter the Sea Trout, *a children's book, and* Time Touch Me Gently, *second-place winner of the Governor General's Award for Poetry in 1967 (Margaret Atwood won first place). Mel passed peacefully at the age of 80. Diana lives in southern Canada. Her first children's book,* Hippos, *from Kidhaven's Animal Attacks series, was published in the fall of 2003. She can be found online as Angel Publications at http://members.rogers.com/angelpub.*

38. Always There When I Need Him
Jessica Bougher

My father died when I was 14, after a brief but horrid battle with cancer. Following his death, my mother, brother, and I went on with our lives. I was angry and resentful that my father had been taken away. Recently, during the last five years, I have begun to "see" my father.

Christmas was always one of my father's favorite holidays. He loved all the lights and decorations, as well as the holiday music. Each year, he tried to outdo what he'd done the previous year with his outdoor decorations. I remember the year that he used branches from a live Christmas tree to create a giant wreath on the garage door, complete with lights and a bow.

He was rather particular about his Christmas trees as well. Because my mother is extremely allergic to live Christmas trees, we always had an artificial tree. Twenty years ago, an artificial tree that looked realistic was hard to find, but he managed to find the perfect tree. He insisted on hanging the tinsel by himself, one strand at a time. We never had light bulbs missing, nor did we spend hours on end untangling Christmas tree lights that had been put away in haste.

As an adult, I cherish the memories of Christmas with my father. Now that I am a parent, I understand the importance of keeping the fantasy and wonder in this very special holiday. With the memories of Christmases past to guide me, I strive to make every one more memorable than the last. It was with those memories fueling my desire for a new Christmas tree to go in the great room of my new home that I spent three days, driving from store to store, trying to locate the Christmas tree that I had decided I had to have. I had been to every major discount retail store in the northeast Atlanta metropolitan area. My search was coming to a grinding halt as I was told, once again, that my desired tree was sold out. I was explaining this to my daughters as we were preparing to leave that department when I saw him.

My father was standing at the end of a row of pallets stacked to the ceiling with every kind of Christmas tree imaginable, except the one I wanted. I was not sure that I was seeing what I thought I was seeing. I had been thinking a lot about him in those days before Christmas, especially when I was having no luck finding the tree that I wanted. I tried to catch up to this man, believing that once I did, I would find that he was a real, live man and most definitely not my father.

The mystery man turned down another aisle of pallets stacked to the ceiling with boxes. When I reached the end of that aisle, I could see him kneeling at the far end examining the label on a box. I was not sure what to do, so I called out and asked if he worked there. The man stood and turned away. I began to walk down the aisle, believing that he had not heard me. As I approached, he turned back to look at me and gestured toward a large box on the bottom of the stack that was pulled a few inches out from the wall of boxes. The numbers on the box were the same as the model number for the tree that I had been desperately seeking. I was astonished. I turned to thank the man, and he was gone. My dad had joined me in my pursuit of the perfect Christmas tree!

The next time I saw him was on a long, hot road trip from coastal North Carolina to Atlanta. I had been visiting my grandparents in North Carolina and taking my children to visit for a few weeks that summer while I attempted to sort out things in my life. My husband and I were recently separated. I had also been recently diagnosed with Multiple Sclerosis, which meant that the career I had built for myself as a landscape designer and contractor was now a thing of the past. I was considering going to Canada to look for a job in a cooler climate with fewer memories.

My grandparents were glad to see my daughters and to see me, until they found out that I was divorcing the girl's father and planning to move to Canada. I left before I said something everyone there would have regretted. On the way out of town, I stopped at the cemetery where my father was buried. Usually, my grandfather went with me to help me find the plot where my father was located. That day, I was on my own. I spent two frustrating hours in the hot sun searching for the marker. I realized that I would never find it and decided to get on the road to Atlanta.

I cried for a while on the way home and decided that it had not been meant for me to find the grave or to leave the silk flowers I had purchased on the grave. I began to put as many miles as I could between myself and the pain of the past. I stopped in the small town where we had lived when my father died. Needing a break from driving and from the heat, I decided to see if I could still find the old neighborhood. I not only found the old neighborhood, but our old home as well.

I was sure that the heat was causing me to hallucinate when I saw my father on the front porch, sitting in his pajamas and robe in an aluminum lawn chair. The pajamas were his favorites—white with blue bi-planes on them—and his robe was chocolate brown terry cloth with beige trim. He was wearing his blue quilted, lambs-wool-lined bedroom shoes with the brown non-slip soles. His hair was thin as it had been the last time I saw him alive, thin because of endless courses of chemotherapy and radiation treatments. His face was gaunt and pale, but not lifeless. His eyes were hazel and seemed to be clear and very expressive.

I wanted to run to him and hang on to make sure that he never left me again. I knew that doing so would only make this miracle disappear. I got out of my truck and stood there for a while, drinking a soda from my cooler while he stayed in his chair. Finally, I got up the courage to speak to him. I wanted to tell him about all of the things in my life that had occurred in the 20 years since he had been taken away from us. I didn't know where to start. Finally, I just blurted out the one thing that I was most sure of, "Daddy, I miss you."

This seemed to lubricate my thoughts and allow me to formulate the things I wanted to say, what I needed to say. The words seemed to come easily, and the answers from Daddy seemed to be there before I could complete each thought. I stood there beside my truck in the driveway, not sure if what I was experiencing was real or only a hallucination brought on by a pending heat stroke.

In the blazing summer sun, I poured my heart out to my father. I felt as though I was only 10 years old and my daddy was there to fix all that was wrong in my world. I knew that he could do nothing to change things in my life. He did help, though. He listened to what I had to say. He didn't criticize my decisions and actions. He made suggestions about some of the issues, saying that I should try to see them from another perspective. About other things, he nodded and said nothing. When he did that, I felt validated in my decisions and beliefs.

When I had vented all of my fears and frustrations, I felt empty, but very peaceful inside. My father told me that it was time for me to leave. I needed to go home and sort things out. He told me that he was never far away, but that I was the only one who could make changes in my life. If I wanted things to change, then I had to change the way I was doing things. Otherwise, nothing would ever improve.

I left wondering if I had really seen and talked to my father, or if I had just imagined it. I decided that it didn't matter. I had needed my father. I needed to talk to him. I needed to see that he still loved me. I found all of those things that hot summer day.

I have never questioned the existence of a world beyond this physical world in which we live. I just wish that we had better ways to communicate with those on the other side.

Jessica Bougher is the author of The Empath's Pocket Survival Guide, Boo! and The Big Yellow Ball, *and* More than Coffee, *and the soon to be released* The Sensitive Individual's Survival Guide *and* Grounded, The Essential Guide to Getting Grounded and Staying Grounded. *She lives in Gainesville, Georgia with four dogs, five cats, a fish, and a snail. You can read more about Jessica at http://www.geocities.com/jessica0402.*

39. The Toy in The Boot
Jon Huntress

I woke up when the car was skidding sideways. I could hear rocks being thrown up against the wheel wells and undercarriage, and then we were rolling. I was bouncing around inside our small station wagon like a brick in a dryer. I had thought the inside of a car would be softer. It hurt a lot, and I wondered when it would stop because it seemed to go on for a very long time. At one point, I watched my own face rise up from the left, look me in the eye, and then disappear to the right. This didn't seem strange.

The next thing I remember was scrambling out of the open tailgate. The car was upside down, and I crawled through a rain of gas from the leaking tank above me. Then there were people all around me, telling me not to move. I could hear my wife, Cherie, talking and yelling from some distance away. I asked the people to help our son, Jesse. I had been asleep in the back of the car with him. We were driving from Santa Fe to Oregon to spend Christmas with Cherie's family. It was just after sunrise, December 18, 1976, in southern Idaho.

Then, Cherie and I were in the ambulance together. I told them to leave me and take Jesse, but they didn't. I was in a lot of pain. At the hospital in Burley, they X-rayed me from every angle, gave me a shot and a neck brace, and told me my son was dead.

They rolled me into a room with Cherie. I said to her, "Now we only have each other."

Cherie then said, "Jesse woke up an hour before the wreck. He said, 'I am going to be a bird!' And I said, 'Jesse, I don't want you to be a bird. I want you to be a little boy and stay with us.' He said, 'No. I'm going to be a bird. But whenever you want me, you can go out to the apple tree and look up and call, Jesse! Jesse! and I'll fly down and be a little boy again.'"

In some deep part of myself, I knew this was going to happen, that my son was going to die. Lying on my gurney in the X-ray room, I thought of a dozen things, some going all the way back to my own early childhood. It was very clear that I had always known, somehow, that all of my life had been a preparation for this. But I didn't know I knew. And I also had the absolute knowledge that I couldn't have stopped it or changed it, no matter what. This was meant to be. I was told, in a very powerful way I can't explain, that I must never question Cherie's driving or any circumstances leading up to the accident, ever. I never did.

And Jesse knew, too. In the months before his death, he changed from a normal 5-year-old to someone much older and wiser. Some time the previous fall, I was reading him some riddles in a comic book. Sitting on the fireplace hearth with Cherie, I asked, "What can you hear that makes no sound?"

Without a moment's hesitation, he replied, "My thoughts."

I asked, "What can you see that you can't touch?"

Again he spoke quickly, "Happiness."

The last riddle was, "What can you feel that you can't see?"

He looked up at Cherie and me with a big smile and said, "My love for you."

I looked at him with wonder and tried to imagine what he was growing to be.

Before Jesse was born, I worried about what kind of father I would be, and what kind of changes a child would cause in our lives. Married four years, we were both teaching in the Berkshires in Massachusetts, and I was playing in a bluegrass band at night. I went to Lamaze childbirth classes with Cherie and read the books. Cherie was in labor most of the night before waking me at dawn to tell me it was time. I drove her to the hospital, put on a gown, helped her breathe, and held her hand for several hours. After a half hour in the delivery room, Jesse was born. The moment I first saw him, all my questions and fears about what kind of father I would be were gone. The universe had shifted. From now on, my purpose was not to have a life into which I had to fit a child. Now I had a son, and my new life's purpose was to do anything and everything for him. "Isn't that something!" I thought, with a smile that split my face for the whole day. I went home to tell our friends and family of my new and joyous reduction to servitude.

After the accident, we spent four or five days in the hospital in Burley. We had no broken bones, or cuts, or visible damage. But we walked gingerly, like tentative old people, no longer sure that gravity could be trusted. Our parents had come to be with us. Cherie went into the funeral home to view Jesse's body. I couldn't make myself go. When she got back, she told me that the room was full of light, and she could see that his small body just couldn't hold all that Jesse was now. It gave her a great deal of comfort and peace. My mother told me later that Cherie had stood looking at the small body with a smile on her face, then reached down, as if taking the hand of a child, and said softly, "Come on, Jesse. Let's go."

Our parents drove us to the motel Cherie's mother and father owned in the Columbia River gorge. Someone had put some flowers with a lot of red berries on the dresser in our room. Everyone was very nice, their smiles tight, eyes full of concern.

I heard soft plopping sounds that first night. In the morning, when I put on my boots, I discovered the bottom of one was full of berries. During the night, the berries had fallen off the plant and rolled about two to three feet along the dresser top, parallel to the edge, then fell into my boot at the end. I felt really happy for the first time since the wreck. Jesse loved to put things, usually toys, in my boots in the morning. When I put the boot on and felt the toy, I would shout, and he would dissolve in laughter.

Friends called from New Mexico, offering to go to our house to put away all of Jesse's toys and things. They said it would be

> The universe had shifted. From now on, my purpose was not to have a life into which I had to fit a child. Now I had a son, and my new life's purpose was to do anything and everything for him. "Isn't that something!" I thought, with a smile that split my face for the whole day.

better than coming back to a house full of reminders. We decided to do it ourselves.

We stayed in Oregon for a month before returning to New Mexico. Our house was in Tesuque, just outside Santa Fe, and it was in shambles because we were in the middle of remodeling. I had stripped the walls and insulated. Only some of the new sheetrock was up. But having the house unfinished actually helped. Our lives were undone, and it was fitting that our environment would reflect this.

We got through the first month because we had a lot of help from family, friends, and neighbors. We found out later that one of our friends had started a large prayer circle out in California that held us in light every day. And we did seem to be almost carried through that time. But when we tried to pick up our routine back in Santa Fe, the real grief came, deep and raw and hard.

We had a stained glass studio on the Plaza in Santa Fe then so, on the bad days, we could stay home or go to work, whatever seemed to help the most. But some days, it was all we could do to just put one foot in front of the other. One evening, I was sitting in my chair with an unread book on my lap, feeling as bad as I had ever felt, when I heard a soft sound from the kitchen. The last thing I wanted to do was to move, but I knew I had to. With the weight of the entire world on me, I forced myself up and went into the kitchen. Cherie was huddled in the corner, sobbing quietly. I sat down beside her and held her. There were no words, but it was enough. There is something about grief that is selfish. It is a dark well, perversely comforting to go down into alone. But I knew that if I stayed there, I would somehow be lost. Death is the flat statement of no hope and that we are truly alone. To deny this and to heal, we have to reach out to another.

> *I had been wrong; we do have souls, and death isn't a final end.*

Before Jesse died, Cherie and I were agnostics. But his death gave us several things, several certainties, that we could build on. One was that while he was dead, he wasn't gone. Something of him was still with us, something more than memory or wishful thinking, something that was solid and real. That meant that I had been wrong; we do have souls, and death isn't a final end.

Another was that we had known, on some level, that this was coming. Jesse also knew, as did some others. A college friend of ours had a Tarot card reading from her grandmother. The reading said a child would die, close to you, but not close, and it happens in sevens. The accident was seven months after the reading, seven days before Christmas, and the car rolled over seven times. This friend and her husband were the only people we knew in Idaho. They helped us in the days after the wreck, and told us of the reading. And that meant that some kind of plan was being worked out, and we were part of it. I knew, somehow, that Jesse died for me. I didn't know why, but I knew it was so, and I knew it was important.

We had close friends who I thought would help us a great deal, who were of no help at all, and acquaintances I had only tolerated before who turned out to have an inner strength that amazed us and were only too happy to share. Nothing was as I imagined it would be. No amount of planning would have helped at all.

One morning, Cherie and I were having breakfast and talking about the day. I reached down and put one boot on and was pulling on the other when my toe hit something. Without a word, I took off my boot and held it up to Cherie, then turned it

> After a great loss, a lot of what people tell you is bad advice, but they mean well.

over. A little car fell out into my hand. The house had been clear of toys for a month. It felt like the morning sunlight in the kitchen doubled.

We had followed the advice of our friends and boxed up the toys. It had not helped. Coming home to the toys Jesse would never touch again was hard, but so was not having them. After a great loss, a lot of what people tell you is bad advice, but they mean well. In our grief, we had a heightened sensitivity to feelings. People would say truly awful things to us like, "You aren't going to have another child are you? You know you can't replace him." But we could clearly see the pain they felt for us, and the hard effort they were making to somehow connect and say something, anything, to make us feel better or avoid further pain. They were clumsy and insensitive, but there was nothing to forgive because they loved us and were doing the best they could.

That first year after Jesse's death was very hard, yet also wonderful. There were dozens of experiences like finding the toy in the boot. Some were reminders, like the toy, telling us that the world really isn't as it appears, and others involved paying closer attention to the people around us. Sometimes that can make all the difference. Love and kindness are the antidotes for loss, and we often found it in unexpected places.

One night, Cherie and I were shopping in a department store. We were waiting behind a couple at the cash register. The clerk was having trouble. She kept making mistakes, and it took her some time to get it right. The couple was irritated and walked away indignantly. The woman took a deep breath, smiled, and asked if she could help us. Cherie had been watching her closely, and something was off. Touching her hand, she asked, "Are you all right?" The woman smiled again and said, "Oh yes." But then her face crumpled and she started crying. "No,

I'm not! My son died last week and *I don't know what I'm doing!*"

We knew just how she felt, trying to go through the motions of normality when it seemed that everything of real value has been taken away. We talked with her for

> *Love and kindness are the antidotes for loss, and we often found it in unexpected places.*

15 or 20 minutes, and we cried together. I told her about the toy in the boot. Every other customer in the store went somewhere else for that time. We were like three people on an island. When we left, we knew she had the strength to meet another hour, maybe another day or week, and we were stronger, too.

Everything seemed to be leading us toward church and, when we eventually did go the Sunday after Easter, we found it a great comfort. The hymns and sermons seemed to be directed right to us. I have two degrees in history, and I had always been leery of Christianity, knowing how bad much of its history has been. But now, I was looking at it again from a different perspective than history can give. When I was in junior high, there was a Baptist church across the street from the school with a neon sign on the side that said "Christ died for you." I never understood that then or later, but now I was starting to get the idea.

Tesuque is a lovely little valley with a small river running through it. There are beautiful black-and-white magpies and large flocks of several hundred large, gray birds that eat the piñon tree nuts in the surrounding hills. One cold afternoon, I was working outside, sanding boards that were going to be the wainscoting for our living room. The boards were rough-sawn timber from the sawmill. I had cut them to size and was sanding them smooth. I was intent because, if you aren't focused with power tools, you endanger the wood and yourself. This was repetitive, boring work, and I was talking to myself. I had taught myself the art of stained glass and now I was learning how to build a house. "Well, here I am, the carpenter." I said. "Just like Jesus, except I've got a belt sander."

What happened next will stay with me always. One of the large flocks of birds was overhead. I was not aware of them; the sander made a lot of noise and my eyes were on the workbench. As I spoke the last word, the entire flock dived down and surrounded me. They were flying all around me, inches from my face, under my legs and arms, around and around me they flew, a swirling avian caress, then up and away, and off to the east and the mountains. I watched the flock until it was just a small darkening in the sky, then carefully put the sander down and walked under the apple tree at the corner of the house to tell Cherie.

We usually don't know how the things we say and do affect others over the long term. But every now and then, something comes back. We never saw the woman at the department store again. I told the story of the toy in the boot in public only once. Writing it now is the second time I have told the story to more than one or two people at a time.

The inspirational author and radio host, Hugh Prather, is a friend of mine. Cherie and I met him and his wife, Gayle, when they wanted stained glass windows for the house they were building in the early 70s. In 1981, Hugh started a new church in Santa Fe and, as soon as I heard about it, I went. The church met at the Girl's Club, and they didn't have anybody to do the music. I brought my guitar the next Sunday and ended up doing most of the music from then on. It was in that church that I found I could begin writing songs about my experiences, six years after Jesse's death.

In the summer of 1982, Hugh and his friend, Jerry Jampolsky, went to Atlanta to help the mothers of the slain children when the serial killer was loose there. He asked me to speak at the church on the Sunday he would be gone and to just tell about Jesse's death, and all that came from it. Hugh was popular in Santa Fe. Most of the congregation knew he was out of town and stayed away. Only about 30 people were there. One woman had come all the way from San Francisco to hear Hugh. When she found he wouldn't be speaking, she was dismayed and almost left. She again thought of leaving when she learned I would be talking about the death of my child. Against her better judgment, she stayed.

When she got back to California, she told a friend the story of the toy in the boot. Sometime later, she heard the terrible news that her friend's son had just committed suicide. "I want you to know," her friend told her later, "that the only thing keeping me alive right now is that story you told me of the toy in the boot."

I didn't find out about this until 10 years later. I was asked to speak at another church, and the woman who introduced me was the same one who had listened to me speak years before. She is a therapist and has since used the story in her work, sharing it with thousands of people.

The unusual happenings we experienced lessened after that first year. They were our lifelines when we were so fragile. Our daughter was born a little less than a month before the anniversary of Jesse's death, and our second daughter two years later. They are the lights of my life.

I remember a quote from one of the many religious books I read back then: "Every bush is a burning bush, if we but have the eyes to see." The world tells us love is a rare and fleeting thing, hard to find, and even harder to keep. "They leave us, on a lonely road. And the armor I wear, is full of holes." is a verse in one of my songs. But there is another reality, very close to us, where love heals everything.

I still watch the birds and listen for the song behind the world I see. There is a plan you know, and I am part of it. We are all part of it. Jesse showed me.

Jon Huntress, the father of two beautiful young ladies, was born in Iowa, but spent most of his life in New Mexico. He holds degrees in American History, Special Education, and Computer Information Systems, and has taught in private and public schools and college. Jon also had a stained glass studio and designed and built solar homes in the Santa Fe area. He was a Y2K consultant and now consults on Internet marketing. He is also a writer and editor for several online companies. Jon currently lives in Houston where he just released his new CD, **Songs That Made Me Cry.**

Jon's CD is available at the following websites:
http://www.MyTexasMusic.com/jonhuntress
http://www.LyricalLine.com/jonhuntress

"What I like about Jon's songs is that he speaks of the power we have to endure and find ways to be here and now. He touches the fabric of what life really is—a continual process of learning to live with uncertainty. He sings of more sensitive ways to relate to ourselves and the world."
-Eric Darling, the Weavers and the Roof Top Singers

About Angela Hoy

Angela Hoy is the author of eight non-fiction titles. She and her husband, Richard, are the owners of WritersWeekly.com (a site that publishes free paying markets and job listings for writers) and Booklocker.com (a publisher of print and electronic books).

Angela and Richard live on the Penobscot River in Bangor, Maine with their four children, Zach, Ali, Frank and Max.

Neither Angela nor her daughter are experienced (and certainly not practicing!) mediums and are not pursuing that line of work. If you wish to contact a licensed medium, please contact the National Spiritualist Association of Churches at http://www.nsac.org/churches or the Worldwide Directory of Spiritualist Churches at http://www.lighthousespiritualcentre.ca/Churchdirectory.html.

Do You Have a Story to Share?

If you'd like to contribute to Angela's next book in this series, or would like to read the experiences of others, participate in discussions, or learn more about spirit communication, please visit her website today at http://www.SpiritStories.com.

Buy you and your pet a nice present today, one that will make your tails wag vigorously!